I ONLY HAVE TIME TO LOVE YOU ON SUNDAY

I ONLY HAVE TIME TO LOVE YOU ON SUNDAY

DE HAGE MINNER

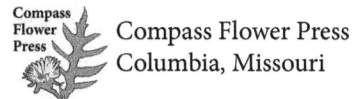

Compass Flower Press
Columbia, Missouri

© 2024 Donna Hage Minner

All rights reserved. No part of this book may be reproduced or transmitted in any form or by any means, electronic or mechanical or by any information or storage and retrieval system without permission in writing from the author or publisher.

Original cover painting by Jenny McGee. Used with permission.

Published by
Compass Flower Press
Columbia, Missouri

Library of Congress Control Number: 2024917864

ISBN: 978-1-951960-65-0

To my family—
those who raised me to adulthood:
Mom, Dad, George, and Mike
And to those who continue to help me grow:
Bob, Angie, and Joe

INTRODUCTION
AUGUST OF 2021

I just made a stranger cry. I was strolling in downtown Cooperstown, New York, today when I came upon a young mother and father with four boys. The youngest appeared to be about six. I noticed he had Down syndrome. "Excuse me," I said to the mother, "is this your little boy?" She said yes but seemed surprised by my question. "I have a daughter with Down syndrome," I continued, "who is forty-seven. She has a wonderful life! She works, she plays, she volunteers and has so many friends and activities—a wonderful life!" The mother started tearing up as she thanked me three or four times for telling her that. Her face told me that she had wondered many times what a future life could possibly be like for this sweet dark-haired little boy. As we walked away from each other we waved and blew each other a kiss. Two mothers with hearts along the same path, one a little farther down the road.

I was a month short of twenty-five, and my husband, Bob, was twenty-nine when our Angela Marie was born. Angie was our first child and the first grandchild on either side of the family. It's not what anyone ever expects, but when it's your first child, it's a real shock. She had serious heart problems along with a myriad of other health issues. How can you even think of what the possibilities or milestones are when you don't have a reference point?

We had no idea what she would be doing at age two or sixteen, let alone at forty-seven, her age now as I start to write our story. Would she even be alive? Let me tell you, she is alive and well and has amazed us all.

Someone once asked me what I struggled with most. It was the looks of pity that we sometimes received, and it was the stereotypes that persisted. It's for this and several other reasons that Bob and I always stop to say something to families we see with children like Angie. I did feel overwhelmed and, yes, angry at times. Not at this sweet baby, but at the circumstances that I felt were thrust upon us. I did some babysitting as a teen for children and babies. Babies who progressed with ease, and children who could walk and talk and let me know what they needed. I watched my friends giving birth around the same time we had Angie, to "perfect" children, with no worries about health or cognition. Bob and I were happy for our friends, but in our own lives, we mourned the clear milestones these babies seemed to meet or exceed. At that point in our lives, we did not understand how much she would teach us.

There were times when Angie was very small and we were struggling, that I would stop and try to connect with a family I saw at the grocery store or at the mall. It did not always end well. I remember seeing an elderly woman in the grocery store one day when Angie was still a baby. At that time, I was grasping for any kind of hope and feeling very alone. I went up to the woman, who had been talking with her adult daughter with Down syndrome. Both looked somewhat disheveled and very tired. I smiled and said hello and that I had a newborn baby like her adult daughter. The woman didn't smile at me. She just harshly said the words, "Good luck," and turned her face away. I was devastated. But who knows what that poor woman and her daughter had to go through. Luckily, that was a different time. The understanding, support, and opportunities are so much greater now. Still, dealing with those internal voices and the looks from others when your child arrives isn't easy for a parent who never expected this to happen. Especially when those around you are celebrating the births and milestones of their "normal" babies. We all need hope, and we all need affirmation that things will most likely turn out okay.

At forty-nine Angie is a beautiful middle-aged woman with innate confidence, a big heart and a smile for everyone, a strong sense of right and wrong, and a great faith and a passion for living her life. She has a housekeeping job that she has worked at and loved for more than fifteen years. She maintains the respect of her co-workers and the love of the elderly people her employer, Tiger Place Independent Living, serves. At times she has even stepped up to lead when others have hesitated.

I heard about one such occasion from another employee. The executive director, Eric, was gone during one of their usual morning meetings. Eric always led the meeting, but when he was away one of the department heads always took the agenda and stepped in. When no one started the meeting, Angie grabbed a copy of the agenda and a pencil, sat up straight, and asked with some authority, "Okay Activities, whadaya got?" After hearing their report and writing what she could of the answer, she went around the table. Nursing? Housekeeping? Food Service? Etc. When Eric came in later that morning, she proudly presented him with the agenda and her notes. When I later asked him about it, wondering if everything was okay, he answered with a positive nod and a big grin.

Angie is one of the most compassionate people I have ever known. Many years ago, when I worked at a nursing home, I would take her to work with me on occasion. It was not uncommon to see her stop when she saw a person struggling, cup their face in her hands, and reassure them gently that everything would be okay. At that time, I was the assistant director of nursing for a large continuing care community. She loved the fact that I had a title. She decided that she needed one also whenever she was there. She dubbed herself the assistant director of smiles, hugs, and weekends. Our family and friends agree she gives the best hugs of anyone we know. Through the years Angie, with her attitude and determination, has helped us understand that everything would ultimately be okay. She has reassured us during times of great concern and helped us to the other side of whatever trauma or difficulty has occurred. Her reaction to the death of loved ones has been a lesson to us.

My youngest brother, Mike, and Angie were very close. Mike was a beloved and attentive uncle to the kids in our family. His crazy antics were legendary, often sending the nieces and nephews into hysterics. Angie adored him, and the feeling was mutual. After a short battle with lymphoma and then a stroke, Mike died when he was forty-six and Angie was twenty-six. When she heard, her grief erupted and seemed to come from the bottom of her soul. She refused to go to the funeral. She was almost inconsolable for about forty-eight hours. She then announced she needed to "get back to my routine." And she did. Work, activities, friends. There was sadness, and occasional outbursts of tears, but she kept going. About three weeks after Mike's death, she walked outside with Bob and me one starry clear night. She scanned the heavens for a few moments and then pointed to a bright star in the sky. "That star right there," she said, "that's Uncle Mike's star!" She had done the same thing when Bob's parents, Bob and Louise, her beloved grandparents, had died (the last family funerals she agreed to attend), and when a favorite cousin, Myra June, had died. The picking of the star has become a ritual, a rite of closure for every close death (including pets) that she experiences.

I hope you will read our story and keep in mind what Angie is today, while understanding that it is as much a story about raising any child, with the ups and downs that occur. Angie happens to have Down syndrome. That diagnosis makes her neither a saint nor an undesirable child. She still got into trouble growing up and also did praiseworthy things with great insight. Both are things we are all capable of. While the diagnosis of Down syndrome and all of her other health issues initially threw us huge curve balls, we have settled into a life full of love and continued discovery. Yes, it has caused us to make special considerations regarding her level of understanding and how we could raise her to be a respectful, responsible, contributing adult, but in many ways, it's been easier than we anticipated.

CHAPTER 1
JULY 1974: AN AWAITED ARRIVAL

As I lay there in recovery, I could feel the flurry of activity and hear the sounds and voices swirling around me, but I could not open my eyes. A male voice cut through the room asking where I was. "She's right here," I heard someone say. "Oh, bless her heart!" the male voice continued. "I'll come back later." Things were starting to come into focus, but nothing looked or felt right. When I asked, a nurse told me we had a baby girl, but her voice seemed flat with little emotion.

I'd had a long labor ending in a cesarean section. I hadn't been worried. My doctor was a well-respected OB-GYN and also a "cousin" of Bob's. But the male voice was not my OB-GYN's. When I could finally see, I asked the nurse who he was. "Dr. Reed, your pediatrician." I knew there was something wrong. The nurse told me I would be going to my room soon and I could see my baby girl then. The waiting room was full of family who were waiting to hear about our new child.

The cesarean section had not been planned, but she was breech. I knew what her name was: Angela Marie. We had decided to keep the chosen names secret from the family so that we could maintain a little control and introduce our baby to all as a named individual. Our parents and some other relatives had driven us to distraction trying to get us to slip up and tell them the chosen names, but we didn't budge! The only exception to this was my maternal grandmother, Taita (an Arabic word for grandmother). She had lived with my mom and dad for the last several summers, coming from her home in Tucson. The last four weeks before Angie was born, she had been in and out of the hospital and her health had deteriorated. I made her promise not to tell anyone else what names we had chosen. She immediately picked up on the name Angela, saying that this would be a very special child. As soon as we had finished our private conversation, she hobbled with her walker into the kitchen and stood beside my mother at the sink. I heard her say, "Ha ha, Nellie! *I* know what the baby's name is and *you* don't!" She died a short time later, two weeks before Angie was born. As I was being wheeled down the corridor to my room, the memory of her words, twinkling eyes, and mischievous smile surfaced in my mind.

Bob was already in my hospital room, and it took no time for a nurse to appear with our sweet baby daughter just as my OB, Dr. Ivan, arrived. As the nurse handed her to me, he explained that he suspected Angie had Down syndrome, a chromosomal abnormality. I told them that I was familiar with Down syndrome. I later went to nursing school, but during this time I was a cytotechnologist, a medical technologist who specialized in cytology or cellular diagnostics. As part of my education, I had learned about chromosomal studies, including those regarding people with Down syndrome. The curriculum included spending time at a school for children with special needs. I remembered fondly the exuberant, sweet spirits and loving hearts of those children we met.

The immediate problem was that she was not sucking correctly, so while I could hold her and love her, I could not feed her for a few days. We finally settled into a feeding pattern that satisfied both the nurses and doctors. In those days, medical practice for a cesarean section dictated that we stay in the hospital for a week. We would make a stop on the way home to see the geneticist. We would need to confirm her diagnosis and find out if Bob and I were genetic carriers (which would likely result in other children with Down syndrome) or if this anomaly was a random occurrence.

It turned out to be random—we were not carriers. One thing I will always remember from that first physician visit was the response of the doctor when he first met us. After being introduced, he took Angie from my arms, rocked her, and cooed to her. He snuggled her and kissed her cheek. He did not seem in a hurry to give her back. His behavior was so affirming to us and helped us focus on the blessing of this beautiful child. We knew we would do everything we could to help her thrive.

CHAPTER 2
A COMPLICATED BEGINNING

The next year was a blur of doctor visits, appointments, diagnostic tests, and therapies. Bob was traveling for his job and often was not home during the week. We resided in St. Louis, where Angie was born, and my parents and in-laws also lived there. I honestly don't know what I would have done without them. My father-in-law or my mother often accompanied Angie and me on doctor visits. Angie was diagnosed with a hole in her left ventricle and several other cardiac anomalies. Cardiac anomalies are a common occurrence in people with Down syndrome (the rate is around 51 percent), along with a myriad of other health problems. Her pediatric cardiologists at Children's Hospital in St. Louis were accessible, kind, and caring. Her relationship with them expanded as the years went by. After the weeks of tests and her concluding diagnoses, they decided that she needed to wait to see if the hole closed on its own, thus avoiding open-heart surgery. She would be followed closely and have regular visits with her Children's Hospital cardiologists.

At eight months old, Angie had not started teething, and although a happy baby, she at times appeared listless. It felt to me as if she was losing ground. She projectile vomited almost every time I fed her. We had been going through months of this; however, she continued to gain some weight. Bob had a new job assignment and was traveling more. I was exhausted and kept trying to tell our pediatrician that there was something wrong, but he just blew it off again and again. "All babies spit up!" he'd say, shaking his head. As a first-time mother with a baby who had special needs I was in a pretty vulnerable place. His demeanor was condescending and made me question my own concerns about the severity of her health problems, and my abilities as a mother.

One day, I noticed a walnut-sized knot in her abdomen. When I pushed on it, it moved. I talked with our pediatrician's nurse. She told me to bring Angie into the office. I was intimidated by the doctor's past patronizing demeanor, so I asked my father-in-law to come with us. As instructed, we stopped for an X-ray before we got to the office. When the doctor walked in, I noted that he was very nicely dressed that day, as if we had interrupted some other plans he had at the time he was seeing us. The dismissive and patronizing look was still on his face. I told him once more about the projectile vomiting and showed him the knot. He bent over, looked at it skeptically, and pushed on it. At the very moment that the knot disappeared, Angie projectile vomited, spewing everything she'd eaten between the openings of the doctor's white lab coat, all over his very expensive suit. He sent us home.

The phone was ringing as we walked in the door. It was his office telling me that the X-ray results had come after we left and showed a weblike duodenal obstruction. Angie needed more tests along with surgery to remove it. It seemed that much of the formula I had so persistently fed her would hit that web and come right back up. But at least enough of the formula was getting through that she was able to gain a small amount of weight. The surgery was rough physically on her and mentally on all of us.

After the surgery there were so many lines attached to her, I could not pick her up or hold her. I sat with my hand in her crib touching her and stayed with her all day long and some nights. I was afraid to leave. Our parents were in and out. Bob was able to stay in the St. Louis office and keep us company most afternoons after work. She spent about two weeks in the hospital recovering.

When we were able to take her home, her projectile vomiting ceased, and as she recovered, her first tooth erupted. Her hair immediately started growing into the most beautiful crop of thick curly brown hair! The thickness of her hair was a complete surprise to us. We had been told that as a person with Down syndrome, she would most likely have thin straight hair.

There was also a noticeable change in Angie's demeanor. Most importantly after her duodenal surgery, she was able to eat and keep her food down. She loved almost everything we gave her, but ice cream was her favorite, and both sets of grandparents, especially her Grandpa Bob, kept her well supplied. Grandpa Bob would take her to Dairy Queen every chance he got. He would come home with a grin on his face and laugh as he told us about all the little happy noises she made after each bite. He called her "Shug," as in sugar.

She smiled and used facial expressions more, started sitting herself up more often, and started to scoot around. She had very lax hip joints and flaccid leg muscles. To sit up she would roll onto her stomach, spread her legs apart, and push herself up with her hands and arms until she was in a seated side splits position. She would then bring her legs around until they were in front of her. We were in awe of the process and amazed at how she ever figured out how to do this. Angie did not crawl until she was about a year old, but she could scoot using her hands, arms, and feet. Bob, an army veteran, thought she looked as if she could have taught trench crawling in basic training. If we were not watching closely enough, we would find her under the buffet or the table in the dining room. She was content until she was locked under the table and could not get around the barrier of the table legs and dining room chairs. We kept an eye on her but also allowed her to explore.

Angie was a very alert, sweet, happy baby. I would often move her with me from room to room seated in her bouncy walking circle on wheels. Her eyes would follow me with connection and anticipation, but she did not use it to walk, only to happily bounce up and down. Her physical progress was slow, and she received physical therapy to strengthen the muscles around her joints. My brother Mike was a physical therapy student, and my brother George had just graduated as an occupational therapist. Both called often to check her progress and were readily available for any advice we needed.

At birth, Angie's middle and fourth finger on her right hand were fused. This anomaly is called a syndactyly. It's not an uncommon finding at birth, and there were people in my family who had been born with a similar condition. We knew that the fingers at some point would need to be separated. The doctors decided to do this at eighteen months. This surgery was so much more complicated than we ever expected. The affected limb was in a cast from her fingertips to up past her elbow, with stainless steel pins sticking out of the tips of her two involved fingers. While the pins were covered with gauze, you could see them and feel them. There was a slight crook in the cast at the elbow. Angie, who was still crawling, became so frustrated during the six weeks the cast was on that she would cry almost every time she tried to crawl. She would go in circles. Finally, when the six weeks were up, we took her back to the surgeon for her cast and pin removal under light anesthetic. After the surgery the surgeon came out to talk with us. She told us the surgery had gone well and Angie's fingers were properly healing, but that she could only find one of the pins. The other pin was missing from Angie's finger. The whereabouts of the missing pin has remained a mystery.

At age twenty months, Angie was still crawling. She was not attempting to pull up yet. I had an opportunity to go back to work in a lab at a newly built hospital, for doctors with whom I had previously worked. The opportunity was a good one, and I felt like I needed a break and Angie needed some socialization. While it was not full time, it was four days a week. I needed to find a babysitter for Angie. That thought alone gave me pause and caused me to question whether this was a good idea. I decided that I would attempt to find a sitter before I accepted the position.

The search alone would help me decide. I started calling the numbers in the babysitting ads I had seen in the paper (remember, this was 1976!). The first two seemed promising until I told them about Angie, her diagnosis and health issues. The first hung up on me; the other politely declined an in-person interview. My heart was sinking. I tried a couple more numbers with no success. The next day I called an in-home day care that was a little farther away in a neighboring suburb. The woman I talked with was named Shirley. When I told her about Angie, she paused, then asked when I would like to come and see her home and interview her. She suggested that I bring Angie and come when the other children she took care of were present.

Oh my goodness she was lovely! We connected immediately when she took Angie from my arms, sat down in the living room, and snuggled her. The five other children were playing within sight, two out in the backyard and the others in the house around a table drawing and coloring. The house was calm, and the kids were smiling and laughing. There was a little dog who seemed very curious about Angie and kept jumping on Shirley's leg. Before I could say anything, Shirley put Angie down on the floor. The dog took off down the hall and Angie followed in hot pursuit, crawling at a clip that I had not seen before. When I picked her up she wanted to get back down on the floor.

I accepted the lab position I had been offered and officially went back to work. It was nine miles to Shirley's and nine more miles to work, but since it was part time, I could make it work. It was the right move. Angie socialized and grew at Shirley's. She actually said her first word there. Shirley had readily available snacks for the kids, usually home-baked cookies and fruit. At home, Angie would point to what she wanted, and we would all jump to get it for her. Shirley lovingly told her each time she pointed that she needed to tell her what she wanted. After a couple of weeks of this cuing from Shirley, Angie pointed and said, "Hoookee!" Her own version of cookie, but it worked. When I picked Angie up that day, Shirley could not wait to show me. It took some coaxing, but she said it! She was promptly rewarded with cookies and hugs. It was repeated for Dad and both sets of grandparents that week. Her words started to come after that. The next words? "Dada," then "Mama."

Our son, Joe, was born when Angie was almost two and a half. She still could not walk because of very lax hip joints, but she was a speed-crawler! We had always planned for more children, and we reasoned that a sibling would help her learn skills and would provide a loving partner to help her navigate growing up. What we didn't bargain for was how much Joe, Bob, and I would learn from her.

When we brought Joe home, Angie took one very sweet and wondrous look at him and kissed him on the forehead. She then crawled away, grabbed a wooden block, and threw it at him. This princess was not used to competition. After all, she had been the first grandchild on either side of the family. We could not leave him on a pallet on the floor because she would crawl over top of him. Over the next few weeks, she gradually lost her complete disgust for the newest member of our family and became his fan and protector. She would sit very close and watch him, kiss him gently on the forehead, and put her toys on his blanket. She would laugh when he laughed, and Lord help us when he cried!

After Shirley was no longer able to keep Angie and Joe, other wonderful sitters appeared in our lives. One right in our neighborhood! Our friend Debbie knew both of our kids well, and her husband, Wayne, worked with Bob. Another, Henrietta, was the mother of a high school acquaintance of Bob's. We were again blessed with people we felt completely comfortable with looking after and loving our children.

Most parents of toddlers and babies are sleep-deprived, and we were no exception. Bob was still traveling a lot. I decided to take a couple of months off work. The doctors where I had previously worked called and asked if I would work at home until I was ready to come back to the hospital. I agreed to help them out since they said they were shorthanded. They brought me a microscope, and each day a courier would bring me folders of slides to read and sign off on while the kids napped.

One day I could hardly keep my eyes open. When the kids were down for a nap, instead of working, I lay down on the couch. Just for a few minutes, I told myself. I was sound asleep when the phone rang in the kitchen. It jarred me awake, and I jumped up, stumbled sideways, landed on my leg that was still asleep, and fell on the floor. I was still not fully awake when I crawled to the kitchen and answered the phone. Was it a doctor's office? Was it work? Please don't wake the kids!

"Hello, Mrs. Minner," effused the overly excited female voice, "we want to let you know that as parents of a new baby we have a wonderful gift for you and your husband. Free dance lessons at Arthur Murry Dance Studio!" I couldn't find words and just hung up the phone. I pulled myself to a sitting position with my back against the wall. I sat there laughing/crying, praying that neither my mother nor my husband nor anyone else would come walking in and find me there on the kitchen floor.

When Angie was about three years old, we registered her at the local regional center. We needed to get her into the state system so that she could receive any services available to her. I was so worried that we would miss opportunities to help her if we didn't start at an early age. Before she could walk, she attended preschool classes with other children with a variety of special needs. She loved the interaction and the activities. The regional center registration brought home visits from a teacher who came every couple of weeks to bring educational activities and gauge her progress in development. While the teacher and Angie sat on the couch working on her developmental skills, baby brother Joe would pull up and stand at the coffee table listening to every word. The teacher started bringing him educational toys to play with while she was there, and when she read the children's books she brought, Angie would cuddle on one side of her and Joe on the other. He looked forward to her visits as much as Angie did. The grant-funded visit program lasted until Angie was about five and Joe three. When it ended, Angie and Joe had progressed from educational play and identifying objects to recognizing their names and knowing their letters and some of their numbers. Joe could recognize words enough to read some of the very simple children's books.

I got a set of magnetic alphabet letters that Angie and Joe could play with on the bottom of the refrigerator. I had seen play desk toys with magnetic letters that had cards with a picture of an object or animal and cut-out spaces for letters that spelled its name. I made card cutouts of Angie and Joe's names with their pictures. I put little magnets on the back of the cards so they would stay on the fridge. The kids both loved the magnets, and I found myself constantly making new cards. I would cut out little pictures from magazines to use with simple words. This was a great activity as long as all the letters remained on the refrigerator! I love running around barefoot, and stepping on these hard plastic letters was very painful!

Joe took off running one day when he was just about a year old. Angie was three and a half and still crawling. She watched his every movement, and her Joe radar constantly tracked him. She started pulling herself up on coffee tables, taking a step while holding on, then she would let go and just drop to the floor. One day when Bob was at home we decided to see if we could help her along. We lined up three of our heavy dining room chairs across our family room. We stood her up at one end while Bob sat on the fireplace hearth with his arms outstretched. He encouraged her to come to Daddy from the chairs, a length of about five feet with nothing but carpeted floor. She went back and forth on the chairs. We could tell she wanted to let go and walk to him, but she would stop short. Then baby brother Joe got into the act. Grabbing the far chair, he went high-stepping across the room in a forward pitch, touching each chair as he went streaking by, right into his father's arms! Bob grabbed him up, and we yelled, clapped, and cheered with Angie standing there watching. Bob sat Joe down on the hearth, and both held their arms open to her.

Suddenly she took off, wobbled the five foot distance, and fell forward into Bob's arms! I started to cry, then I realized that both Bob and Angie were crying too. He picked her up and placed her back at the chairs, and she did it again and again, crying the whole time.

We called her grandparents to tell them the great news and then went out for ice cream! We had gone in a matter of a week from having a three-and-a-half-year-old and a one-year-old, with neither one walking, to both of them walking! It's amazing how parents need to constantly readjust to different stages of a child's life. They also must adjust differently to each child. It can be intuitive and challenging at the same time. That year, Bob proudly walked both Angie and Joe around to the neighbors for Halloween.

By this time, Angie and Joe were inseparable. They could also get into so much trouble together. Bob usually watched the kids while I cooked dinner. One night they disappeared. We could hear noises and giggles from the bathroom at the end of our long hall, but the door was closed. When we pushed the door open Angie grabbed the counter and pulled up on her toes and turned the light off. When we turned it back on, both kids were wide-eyed, running in place with nowhere to go. I realized that there was something shiny and foamy all over the carpet, the sink, the tub, and the cabinet. As I stepped onto the carpet in my stocking feet there was a warm squish, and I felt something wet wicking up through my socks. When I tried to pick up the potty chair, it slid out of my hands and hit the floor with another louder squish. There were large (but empty!) bottles of baby oil and baby shampoo lying in the middle of the floor. The kids had emptied them all over the carpeted floor and had used the bathroom towels to spread the greasy mess on every surface. We cleaned and wet-vacuumed, but for months, every time one of the kids missed the potty chair, or the carpet got wet, bubbles would appear.

When Angie was close to five, the cardiology office called and asked us to come in for a test. The hospital had purchased a new dimensional ultrasound, and the doctor thought it would be helpful to use it with Angie. Since Children's Hospital in St. Louis is a teaching hospital, and the technology was new, there were several residents present, along with the ultrasound techs, cardiologists, nurses, and attending physicians. Angie was frightened by the machine and the crowded room. We had developed the habit of singing a specific song when she felt ill at ease, so she and I softly started singing while she lay there on the table. "Where oh where are you tonight? Why did you leave me here all alone? I searched the world over and thought I found true love, but you found another and POOF you were gone!" It was a song from the old TV show *Hee Haw*. She loved to sing that song, and it seemed to calm her. By the time the test was finished, almost every voice in the room had been added to the chorus. The residents, the attending physicians, the techs, the nurses, Angie, and I were all singing the *Hee Haw* song over and over in unison. She loved it. I can only imagine the number of earworms that existed in the halls of Children's Hospital for the rest of that day.

After the ultrasound the doctors became increasingly concerned about Angie's heart. Shortly after she turned five, we started noticing a duskiness around her lips. We realized that at times she was using her neck muscles to breathe. She sat a lot more and didn't walk with the same intent or excitement that she had before. Her cardiologists told us it was time for surgery. What they had thought might heal itself had not. They noticed that her heart pressure seemed to increase when she lay down. Her oversized tonsils were identified as the culprit, and a plan was formulated. She would have her tonsils removed and go home for two weeks. She would then come back to the hospital for open-heart surgery to repair the quarter-sized hole between two chambers of her heart using a Teflon patch. Her tonsillectomy went by without a hitch. On the way home two days after surgery, she wanted a soda and potato chips.

I thought about sending her back to preschool for the two weeks in between surgeries just to provide us all with some normalcy. But there was an outbreak of scabies at her preschool, and we couldn't take the chance of having her surgery delayed. We spent the next two weeks living within ourselves as a family, playing, taking drives, cuddling, and staying away from anything that might keep her from having her open-heart surgery.

The day before the surgery Angie was admitted to the hospital, and the nurse navigator came to talk with us. She sat us down to go over everything and help us prepare. We had been told to bring Angie's favorite doll. Mary was a well-worn rag doll missing a few stitches, and Angie slept with her and took her everywhere. The nurse explained that Mary would undergo everything that Angie would before she did. They would take Mary to get tests and go to surgery, then bring her back to the room after each test or surgical event. When Mary had blood tests, she came back with a Band-Aid on the inside fold of her elbow. Mary went for X-rays and came back sitting up in a wheelchair. The night before Angie went to the operating room for her open-heart surgery, Mary went to open-heart surgery and came back on a gurney with a "chest pack" and drainage tubes taped to her chest, just like Angie would. Angie watched intently and with great curiosity as all of this happened to her beloved Mary. We had explained her surgery to her in simple terms the best that we could. The nurses and I continuously praised Mary, and with every step we expressed to Angie how well Mary was doing.

The nurse navigator told me that Angie would look like she had been hit by a truck when I first saw her back from surgery, and she did. She was colorless, with a terrified "What in the world just happened?!" look on her face. She was wheeled immediately into the cardiac intensive care unit (CICU), and an oxygen tent was affixed to the top half of her bed. By the end of the day, she was starting to sit up. There was a constant stream of medical residents in and out of her space, and you could tell that she did not like any of them one bit. They interrupted her sleep, prodded her and poked her dressing, listened through stethoscopes, made her move. She got so she would act like she was asleep in the tent if they approached. After she didn't need the tent, the nurses realized that it had become a safe haven for her, so they affixed it to the foot of her bed with the opening toward the head. If she saw the residents coming, she would often duck in, turn her back to them, and refuse to come out. She was in the CICU for several days, longer than they usually keep people because of stridor caused by the intubation, and an anaphylactic reaction she had while eating lunch. We still don't know what caused the anaphylaxis. We carried an EpiPen for years, but it has never happened again.

When she went to a regular hospital room we were thrilled. She slept better, ate better, and was less anxious. I had given her a pad and colored pencils to draw with. After working on it for a little bit she handed it back to me. Just as plain as if I had written it myself were an A and a B. She had been working on her letters in preschool before the surgery. One of the things we had feared would happen because of the surgery had not—Angie hadn't lost any of what she had previously learned.

Before we went home Angie asked to see Mary, her favorite doll. Mary had been shoved in a heap in the corner of the windowsill, and Angie refused to sleep with her anymore. She grabbed Mary with both hands, tore her already loose arm off, and slammed her into the trash can, chest pack, tubes, and all. Angie thought Mary was somehow the cause of all that she had been through in the past couple of weeks. No amount of explaining or dissuasion could change her mind. I retrieved Mary without Angie knowing and kept her for a long time. I think this had something to do with my own healing from Angie's trauma.

Having an extended hospitalization and multiple serious surgeries can have an effect on anyone, but we never realized how much it had on Angie until the following months after she had been discharged from the hospital. We took her and Joe to the zoo after she had recuperated at home for a while. We thought it might be a fun outing, and it was! We had a great time. When we came upon the lemur exhibit there was an area full of trees with several ring-tailed lemurs in view. Angie took one look, got very excited, and yelled, "Look, there's a lactated ringer!" (A hospital IV solution.) It's what we've called them ever since.

We had given her a toy doctor's kit before surgery. We played with it beforehand and made light of taking vitals, listening to her heart and lungs, giving shots, etc., hoping this would help her be more familiar with having her vital signs taken so often at the hospital. We did not realize how much more important it would become to her after the surgery than it was before. When she got home, it was one of the first things she grabbed from her toy shelf. She made rounds for weeks on any adult sitting still long enough for her to listen to their heart, test reflexes and, lastly and most ceremoniously, give them a shot. When she gave the shot, she would poke the fake plastic syringe into your arm as hard as she could until you said, "Owww!" (Yes, it hurt!) She would then start crying and hug you and tell you that you would be okay, that it was just a little shot. This went on for a few months before she gradually went on to other unrelated things. When I think of all that she went through and the unavoidable trauma that was necessary for her life to continue, it puts a lump in my throat. I am still amazed about how tough she was throughout all of this, and at such a young age.

A residual effect from Angie's open-heart surgery that lasted for a few years was the stridor that occurred due to her intubation during surgery. Stridor is basically an inflammation of the larynx caused by pressure from the tube. Angie would wake up in the middle of the night with breathing difficulty and a high-pitched wheeze. Either Bob or I would pick her up and run outside with her into the cool night air or go into the bathroom and turn the hot water on full force to create a steam bath. My parents would be called to come and stay with Joe, or we would drop him off on the way to the emergency room. It was all so rushed and frenetic in our attempt to get her there before she couldn't breathe at all. Once there, they would give her epinephrine in an aerosol mask, and her breathing would ease. They always kept her for observation, and we would sit for hours in the emergency room while she slept on a gurney. After this had happened a few times, Angie knew the drill. She would come into our room to tell us. Once at the hospital, she knew exactly what was happening. If a doctor or nurse faltered in the order of assessment or treatment, she would tell them. ("You forgot my temperature!") Holding out her hand, Angie would grab the mask from them, putting it up to her mouth and nose before they could place the strap around her head.

Joe knew the drill too. He was three when Angie had her open-heart surgery, and around seven when Angie had her last stridor episode. It amazed us how he adapted to this abrupt awakening, being pulled from his bed in the middle of the night. He would get up without question or fuss, hug his stuffed monkey, and watch us calmly as we got dressed, ran in and out of the bathroom or in and outside with Angie, and made arrangements with Taita and Jiddo (the Arabic words for grandfather) for his care.

Joe seemed to have a watchful eye at a very young age, especially when he was around Angie. He often sensed what she needed. One day when he was about four, he told me he wanted some envelopes and white paper. He had also asked for an empty egg carton. After he and Angie had spent a couple of hours in Joe's bedroom, he asked me to come to see what he had done. He had drawn a four-year-old's version of five houses. Each was outlined in a different crayon color, with a very large number in the middle of it, one through five. Each house picture was standing separately propped up on his bookshelf with spaces in between. He excitedly told me to watch as he handed Angie the white envelopes marked with corresponding numbers. He turned to Angie and half yelled, "Angie, you're the mailman and you have to deliver the mail!" She took each of the envelopes, looked at the number, and one by one found the house picture they corresponded with. She laid each envelope against the matching house number. Joe jumped up and down, yelling, "Yayyyyy!" She grinned as he demonstrated a joy that seemed to brighten the light in the room. Joe also colored the indentations of the egg carton in the same colors that came in a bag of M&M's. He then told Angie she had to sort them and put them in the cups with the right color. When she finished, they sat down and devoured them together, giggling with delight!

One of my fondest memories of these two together was seeing them sitting on the floor in front of the TV with their arms around each other, watching *Sesame Street* and *Mister Rogers' Neighborhood*. They were mesmerized by both shows, and they both learned so much. Joe especially liked learning the Spanish taught on *Sesame Street*. After the show, the two of them would run to the kitchen and clean out two bottom connecting cabinets on the same side, with door openings facing each other.

They would crawl inside, fling the doors open at the same time and yell, "Abierto!" Then, grabbing the inside door magnets, they would slam the doors shut and yell, "Cerrado!" This could go on for an hour. I could usually distract them by preparing a snack and giving it to them while they sat in the cabinet with the doors wide open.

CHAPTER 3
A CALMER TIME

Life had slowed to a manageable pace for us. Our family dynamics were a little more relaxed and routine. The focus was not so much on Angie's health crises but on our family. We made sure that we made individual time for each child. Joe played soccer, and later baseball, while Angie cheered on the sidelines with us. They would spend overnights with friends and with grandparents, the latter both individually and together. We have been asked many times by other parents how to handle making time for their other children. Is it okay to take the others on a vacation doing things that the siblings with special needs might not enjoy or be able to do? Is it okay to take them out separately at times? Our answer is always YES! Both of our kids went to different camps at different times during the summer. Joe to Boy Scout camp, and Angie to an adventure camp for kids who were differently abled. We made it a practice to do things with Joe when Angie was gone that were a little more challenging and focused on him. We would usually, once during the week, take him out for a dinner at a very nice restaurant. He wore a suit; Bob and I got dressed up, and Joe was told he could order whatever he wanted from the menu. We did the same for Angie when he was gone. We wanted them each to spend some time as the sole object of our attention.

When we went out to these dinners, we used the opportunity to have fun and teach the kids about manners, how to relax in a formal setting, and what the expectations were for their behavior in a more formal public place. We also took little trips when one or the other was at camp. These focused events created great memories and were so much fun. Usually one time during the week that Joe was away, Angie and I would have a girls' day of fun and shopping. During one of these outings, we stopped for lunch at a nice restaurant. I watched Angie intently perusing the menu. When the waitress came to take our order, she looked at Angie at asked what she would like to have. Angie looked a little puzzled but took one more look, squinted at the menu, then said to the waitress, "I'll have the—Godzilla burger." The waitress never missed a beat. "And would you like Godzilla (gorgonzola) cheese with that or American cheese?" Exhaling with great relief, Angie said, "American!" I was so taken with the waitress's understanding and immediate response that I later called over the manager and relayed the story.

The day that Angie completely dressed herself for church, without help, was a banner day. She was one very proud and independent nine-year-old. I made her twirl around, checked to see that her slip was not backwards or inside out, and noted that she had the correct shoe on each foot and matching socks. I told her we were very proud of her, and she beamed. We piled into the car and headed for church. We weren't late, but the only open pew left was toward the front. Once we genuflected and knelt for a quick prayer, we sat down. The minute that Angie's bottom hit the cold wooden pew, she started screaming, "Mommy, I don't have any underpants on! Mommy, I don't have any underpants! Mommyyyyy!" I could not quiet her or calm her down. I looked at Joe—he was horrified and had moved several feet away toward the other end of the pew. People around us were staring. I knew we had to leave. I motioned to Joe, but he moved even farther away from us. I asked Joe if he wanted to stay, but he shook his head emphatically no. We filed hurriedly out of the pew with Angie still crying loudly about no underpants. It was the longest church aisle I had ever walked. Once we were back in the car, I went into self-flagellation mode. How could I not have checked to see if she was wearing underwear when I checked everything else? Oh God, did she moon anyone behind us? She had a habit of dramatically flipping her dress up in the air before sitting down.

Bob had not gone to church with us that morning and was sitting at the kitchen table when we got home. The minute Angie saw her dad, she started crying again. When I explained what happened, he sent Angie off to her room to get underpants, put his head down on the table, and made a valiant effort to keep from laughing. When he was able to straighten up, he called Joe over and told him he knew it had to be tough to be there in front of everyone and experience that, but embarrassing things happen to everyone. I think I needed to hear that as much as Joe did. We knew that Angie would be okay. She never seemed to drag yesterday with her to the next day unless it was something good.

We piled back into the car and went back to church, parked in my previous but unfortunately still empty parking spot and walked back in. Of course, the only pew still available was the one we had vacated. Angie led the way, trauma forgotten, with her head held high. Joe and I followed lagging behind. I found myself wondering why we had come back. Then I remembered, today was the Mother's Day market after church that the kids were to attend to buy me a Mother's day gift. Bob would be meeting us there to help the kids. I decided I would take the extra car and head home. After everything that had happened, I needed some quiet time.

Joe was seven years old when he started preparing for his first communion. He came to Bob and me and told us that he wanted Angie to make her first communion with him. We discussed this with Sister

I Only Have Time to Love You on Sunday

Mary, who said she would be happy to tutor Angie. Every week when Joe went to first communion and confession classes, Angie went to see Sister Mary. The first communicants were able to individually pick the date that they would receive their first communion at mass. We planned a party for the kids after mass at our home. Angie had a beautiful white eyelet dress with a little crown of flowers and a veil. Joe had a new blue suit and tie. They looked adorable. We occupied the whole first pew to the right of the middle aisle. Both sets of grandparents were there. Bob's parents were at the far end, mine were next, then Bob, me, Angie, and Joe. I had noticed that Angie seemed a little nervous that morning, but otherwise she seemed fine.

When it came time for first communion, she grabbed my arm and pulled me up to go with her and Joe. I felt a little awkward standing behind them, but I remained. Father said to Joe, "Joseph, this is the body of Christ." Joe said, "Amen," took the communion into his outstretched hands, put it into his mouth, bowed his head, and blessed himself. It melted my heart to see him. Father turned to Angie. "Angela, this is the body of Christ." She hesitated and then mumbled, "That's disgusting!" Father's mouth dropped open a bit; he looked at me, then turned back to her. "Angie, I said this is the body of Christ!" She instantly retorted, "And I said that's disgusting, and I don't want that stuff in my mouf!" Father hesitated again, then for some reason handed me the consecrated host. We turned and filed back into the pew. I was horrified. Joe, after kneeling down and saying a prayer, looked up at me and said, "Mom, just tell her it's chicken; she'll eat it!" My mother, from the other end of the pew, whispered forcefully in her usual loud whisper voice, "DeDe, DeDe, let me try—I'll give it to her!" Bob (who is not Catholic) looked over at my dad and asked, "So, is she Catholic now or what?" Bob's parents (also not Catholic) were obviously very confused. In my mind, it was an unexpected nightmare. My mouth went totally dry, and I felt like

I could hyperventilate into my purse. Hadn't she had classes along with Joe? Wasn't Sister Mary tutoring her? Where the heck was Sister Mary?

After mass, Father Rock found me standing in a corner of the vestibule and took me aside. He said, "De, don't let this throw you. Joe did a wonderful job! Angie had her beautiful dress, crown, and veil, she has a party to go to, and when she is ready to make her first communion, she will just make it without all the fanfare. You and I have to worry (about our souls), but she doesn't." His words made such a difference to me. I took a deep breath and then exhaled most of my embarrassment. (Yes, it took me a while to totally get over this!)

Before we left the church that day, someone gave us a little bag with a few unconsecrated communion hosts and told us to just let her get familiar with the taste and feel. I put them in a kitchen drawer and forgot about them. A couple of weeks later, I heard Angie yelling at her brother. Joe had taken the hosts and mixed them into a bag of potato chips and given them to her. She was not fooled or amused.

A few years later, when Angie was in junior high school, she was at my parents' home after school. We had made arrangements for Angie to get off the bus there since I did not get home from work in time to meet her. My mom had just had a revision of a previous knee replacement and was not very mobile. Angie being there also allowed Dad to get out and run errands. Angie could wait on Mom, getting her whatever she needed. One day while she was there, Mom received a phone call that her youngest brother, Bob, had passed away unexpectedly. It made Mom so very sad, but Angie was there to comfort her. Mom called her church and asked that someone come to pray with her. When the deacon came, he brought communion. Angie willingly and reverently received her first communion that day. There with her Taita, and as Father Rock had predicted, without fanfare, and when she was ready. My mom always cherished this beautiful memory that accompanied the sadness of her brother's passing.

When Angie was about ten years old, she announced one day that she wanted her own condo. Bob and I looked at each other and started to chuckle. Not because we were laughing at her dreams. She was such a self-assured young lady, we often chuckled at her sweet hubris. This statement became a sort of mantra over the next nine years. She never let it lie for very long. She would pull it out and fling it up in conversation like a bright balloon tied to a post, whipped in the wind.

She may have wanted her own condo, but she was not willing to let loose of the need for her night-light when she went to bed, even though our backyard light was like a beacon of daylight streaming through her bedroom window. One day when Angie was about twelve, Bob decided it was time to get rid of the night-light. After he kissed her good night and tucked her in, he sat on her bed and dad-splained why the night-light was not necessary. After she could see that her arguments to keep it were proving unsuccessful, she threw her arms around Bob's neck, kissed him repeatedly on the cheek, and frantically patted his back. "No, Daddy, no! Please, please, please! I love you so much, Daddy!" He finally acquiesced and told her okay, it was fine for her to keep it for a while. He then got up, tucked her in, and had one foot out in the hall when we heard Angie mutter under her breath, in a quiet but very different tone, "Poo poo head!" He never did revisit the night-light thing.

I can't tell you why or where it first happened, but Angie became deathly afraid of dogs. If we were on a walk and we encountered a dog, she would start shaking and crying, sit down, and melt limply into the sidewalk, impossible to move. We were so concerned about her behavior that we knew we had to do something. The big question was, what? We tried taking her to the home of friends and introducing her to their pets in a controlled environment, but that did not work. We knew that unless she had a long-term relationship with a dog, nothing would change. One Saturday morning we made a trip to the local dog pound. Angie went with us but chose to stay in the car. We looked at so many dogs, we couldn't make a decision. That is, until they brought us a seven-month-old white terrier mix with black spots and blue eyes. He immediately went over to Bob and Joe and laid down at their feet. He was so calm and sweet, we knew he was the one we wanted to take home. He had been ill with a virus but was recuperating and was deemed ready to leave.

We really had not thought the ride home through very well. It would be interesting with Angie and our new family member in the same car. We decided to put Angie in the front seat with Bob, while Joe and I sat in the back with our new dog on a tight leash. It worked until Joe relaxed his hold on the leash a little when we stopped at a stoplight. The dog somehow wedged his head around the outside of Angie's seat and licked her in the face. We had no idea what had happened until we heard a high-pitched squeal and Angie had pulled herself almost over onto Bob's lap.

After we got home, Angie barricaded herself in her room for a couple of hours. Our new family member lay in the corner of the kitchen surveying his new home. When Angie came out of her room, she went right to the family room, turned on cartoons, and sat on the floor to watch. The dog got up, peeked around the corner, and watched Angie for a moment. He then bolted into the room, and before she knew what was happening, he again licked Angie's face. She let out another squeal and, in a single motion, was up off the floor and seated in her dad's recliner with her legs cranked up and the back laid as far back as it would go. The sweet terrier mix lay down beside her, unfazed by her reaction.

To get her more involved, we decided to give Angie the privilege of naming him. She named him Alf, after her favorite TV show. For a while they gave each other space. Gradually this moved to petting with us holding him and then to their own unsupervised interactions. Alf seemed to understand that Angie needed something totally different than Joe did. Joe and his friends could run and play and roughhouse with Alf, but Alf was always subdued and calm around Angie. She was comfortable with him. You could see his love for both Angie and Joe. At night he would pull an old worn sleeping bag of Joe's out from under his bed and find one of Joe's shoes. He would lie down on the sleeping bag with his head on Joe's shoe and sleep next to Joe's bed. Angie's fear of other dogs did not totally go away, but it turned into more of a wariness. She no longer was so petrified that she cried and sat on the sidewalk, but she would definitely give wide berth to other dogs we met.

CHAPTER 4
JUNIOR HIGH SCHOOL

Anytime there was a change in routine or life for Angie, we worried. When she went to junior high school we were concerned about the new bus ride and the new larger school. Like many of us, she always did best when she was allowed to work within the structure of ingrained routines. The difference with Angie was how she responded when the structure of those routines was changed. She sometimes had trouble adapting. We met and liked her new teachers but knew that this would be a challenge for both them and Angie. What our worry clouded was the fact that Angie was maturing and could handle more than we were willing to admit. She loved junior high school, her teachers, and her new friends. She attended her first school dances and regularly socialized with the other students outside of school.

Telling time was something Angie had been working on for a while. She would bring home worksheets with clock faces and instructions to plot the written time for her homework. Bob, Joe, and I all worked with her, but telling time with an analog clock somehow eluded Angie, until one day she seemed to fix the problem herself. I had noticed her standing in the middle of the kitchen staring at an analog clock that was on one side up over the kitchen table. She would then turn slightly to face the digital clock on the microwave and read the time out loud (luckily, they were synchronized). She went back and forth several times repeating the time on the digital clock while checking to see where the hands were on the analog clock. Something had sparked when she realized they were both telling her the same thing. She was extremely proud that she had figured this out. It also gave us more of an idea of what kind of reasoning she was capable of. Thinking outside the box to help her was something we had to do more of, along with enabling her to utilize her own problem-solving skills.

We lived on a cul-de-sac at the end of a street full of kids and great neighbors. One day shortly after we had moved in, I had gone to the store while Bob was splayed in his recliner taking a power nap, sweaty in his dirty shorts and tee shirt. He'd been working in the backyard and needed a shower but wanted to rest and cool off first. He was half asleep when he thought he heard Angie's voice along with another voice he didn't recognize. He opened his eyes to see a very surprised strange woman standing there almost frozen in place looking down at him. Her hair was sopping wet; she was barefoot and wearing an old bathrobe. The lady and Bob looked at each other in confusion with their mouths open for a second. Angie then piped in, "Carol, meet my dad. Dad, meet Carol!" Carol stuttered, said it was nice to meet him, then added, "Oh my gosh, I am so sorry!" She told Bob that Angie had knocked on her door right across the cul-de-sac. When she answered, Angie said hi and then motioned for Carol to follow her across the street. When Carol, just out of the shower, asked Angie what she needed, she kept saying, "Come here, come here!" Carol told Bob, "I thought something was wrong, so I came!" Bob started laughing and told her it was really nice to meet her, and he was sorry too. Angie had apparently decided that it was time for us to meet some of our neighbors. We laughed about Bob and Carol's meeting for years after that.

Angie has always loved music. From a young age, she had a natural sense of rhythm and loved both singing and dancing. One of her junior high school teachers worked with the children in Angie's classroom to put on a performance for parents and friends for Parents' Day one year. Angie was excited about it but would not tell us what it was or what her role would be. She said she had to "dress nice" for that day, but other than an invitation with the time and date and the words "Class Performance," that was the only information we received. It was the middle of the afternoon, so Bob was not able to attend. My mom was available to come. As we sat in our seats, the children assembled on a two-tiered riser against the wall across from us. When the kids were ready, a cassette player was turned on, and Sandi Patty's song "Love in Any Language" started to play. On cue, the kids stood erect and started crisply and dramatically signing (in American Sign Language) the words to the song. It was beautifully synchronized and so graceful that you could hear quiet gasps from the adults who were present. When they were finished, we were teary-eyed and filled with gratitude for the beautiful performance we had just witnessed. Angie was happy to repeat her performance for her dad, her Jiddo, her grandma and grandpa, and anyone else who would sit still long enough to watch.

We had noticed over the years that Angie had some issues with her visual perception of spaces and heights. Joe loved learning about the presidents, so on a weekend vacation we had taken the kids to Springfield, Illinois, so that Joe could visit the Lincoln monuments. While there, we decided on a whim to tour the Frank Lloyd Wright Dana-Thomas House. The house has multiple levels, requiring steps to go in and out of many of the rooms. By the time we finished the tour,

Angie was inching along with her back flat against the wall and her arms outstretched, groping the wall as she went. She looked with trepidation at each set of steps before she committed to going up or down.

If we took her to a show in a large arena, she would sit plastered against her seat with a white-knuckle grip on the seat arms. To clap, she would let go for a few seconds, clap her hands quickly four or five times, and then immediately reestablish her death grip on the arms. She had, it appeared, the perception that if she let go, she would fall out of her seat. Since our attendance at these types of events was pretty sporadic, we weren't sure how to help her until one summer, friends asked if we wanted to share Cardinals baseball tickets. Bob and Joe were and still are avid Cardinals fans! If we chose to participate, we would have four tickets to twenty games. At first, we thought it would be too much for Angie. The wheels started turning as we discussed it. The seats would be the same each game, in a section that was about ten steps down from the ramp. We inquired about nearby bathrooms and found there were some close by, back up the steps and just around the corner. The consistency and repetition, we reasoned, might help her get past her fear. We were hopeful and decided to see if it would make a difference. We talked excitedly to both kids during the weeks before the season started. How great would it be to see our beloved Cardinals team in person and get to see the players? Angie loved Fredbird, the team mascot. Both kids seemed excited, a good start to the process.

The first couple of games were stressful. Bob sat next to Angie with his arm around her to give her a feeling of safety. She still maintained her death grip on the seat arms, and getting her down and up the steps took both of us. When getting her up the steps for the bathroom, we could still see Joe in his seat. When we got to the top, Bob would then run back down to the seats, and I would take her the rest of the way. She would self-talk her way both up and down the steps, giving herself encouragement and accolades when she finished. If she looked up when coming back down, she would freeze, so we would encourage her to only look at her feet. She started to get more comfortable with each game we attended. Over the next few games, she clapped more, gradually loosened her grip, and finally told her dad she didn't need his help getting up the steps to the bathroom; she could just go with Mom. We had a wonderful time as a family. While we didn't take her to every game, our attempt to help alleviate her fears and change her perception was a success.

Bob, after some years in the corporate business world, left his desk job and started a new business. He went to the bank every Saturday, and Angie loved to go with him. He would stop and get them each a donut after the banking was finished. One day at the bank, lines were especially long, and the tellers were working hard to keep up. At the head of Bob and Angie's line was a man who seemed to be very unhappy with both the teller and the bank. He kept raising his voice and then started yelling and cursing in a loud voice at the teller, who was obviously shaken. Other tellers came over to assist. Bob looked down at Angie. She was wide-eyed, and before he could grab her, Angie ducked through the crowd and made a beeline for the man. Bob said his heart was in his throat as he watched her (well out of his reach) grab this angry man's sleeve and tug on it. The man, surprised by the contact, turned abruptly to see who had grabbed him. When he made eye contact with her, she told him, "Sir, it's not nice to say bad words in plubic!" She then let go and walked calmly through the queue back to Bob. The man just stood there for a few seconds, then resumed his business without cursing or yelling and went on his way. When he left the bank, someone started clapping. She got an ovation and lots of smiles from people in the bank who had been witness to the incident, along with thank-yous and a fistful of lollipops from the tellers.

CHAPTER 5
HIGH SCHOOL

A change in territories for Bob's business moved us to a small town right before Angie started high school and Joe started junior high. It was a difficult freshman year for Angie in a smaller school, but by graduation the school had fallen in love with her, and she had friends everywhere. She was teased by some of the students who didn't know better and those who were reflecting their own internal insecurities. One student named Christy had noticed Angie sitting alone on the school bus and made a special effort to befriend her. She said she wanted others to know how sweet Angie was, and she wrote a lovely article for the school paper, introducing Angie. It helped, but it still took a while for many students to understand how her needs and wants were much the same as theirs.

Angie was in a special needs home room, but there were no other students like her. Most in her home room had learning disabilities, dyslexia, or behavioral disorders. They were not sure they wanted to be associated with someone who had a more obvious disability than they did. Her home room teacher, who was one of the special education teachers, was intuitive and wonderful. Ms. Sue and Angie connected immediately. Her classmates were standoffish when she started, but Ms. Sue wanted the others in the class to understand Angie's abilities and see her as a person. Angie could read around a third-grade level, so Ms. Sue started by having Angie help some of the dyslexic students with word-seek puzzles and reading exercises. Others helped her with counting money. Through this cooperative effort, they got to know her and grew to love her humor and her honesty.

Shortly after we moved, I heard an ad on the radio for a college nursing program. I was already in a medical field, but with all we had been through, I was drawn to the thought of going back to school and becoming a registered nurse. I talked it over with Bob and the kids and decided to go for it. I enrolled in the nursing program of a college nearby. It was one of the hardest things I have ever done for myself, and one of the best. I think I had always been a nurse at heart. The changes in family routine were interesting and difficult, but no one complained. I would go into our extra bedroom and spread out my books and papers on the bed to study. The door would squeak open as both kids would enter, schoolbooks in hand. They would sit quietly on the floor or in the chair and get to work. Our lives were all changing. We were all growing.

Angie and Ms. Sue developed a wonderful relationship outside of the classroom. Angie spent time at her home, and Ms. Sue took on some instruction in other aspects of Angie's life. We had tried to get Angie to learn to swim. However, we didn't realize she needed lessons just to get in the water. Angie getting her ankles wet resulted in a lot of self-talk and self-encouragement. "I know you can do this, Angie! Yes, you can!" She also demanded bribery. When we tried to coax her into the pool, she would inform us, "I get ice cream for this!" We had tales of previously failed lessons. One included a six-foot-three, two-hundred-pound physical education teacher with a very hairy chest who taught swimming in the summer. On their first meeting, after a little poolside chit chat, he picked her up, got in the pool, and started walking toward the deeper water to show her it wouldn't hurt her. When the water got up past her hips, she put a knuckle lock on his chest hair and refused to let go. It was one of the most painful things we had ever witnessed. With a look of sheer agony on his face, he finally had to dunk her to make her let go.

For some reason Ms. Sue, the trusted and patient miracle worker, was able to get her into the pool as long as she could hang onto the side. She coaxed her step by step toward the deep end. When they got to the place where Angie would tread no further, still with her white-knuckle grip on the side, Angie looked down wide-eyed at the water surrounding her chest. She then looked up and blurted, "I'm shrinking!" Ms. Sue gently assured her she was not, and they started step by step back to the shallower end. We could see that with Ms. Sue, the genuine love and trust that had developed between them greatly affected Angie's openness to learning new things.

Since school is about both educational learning and workforce preparation, we were happy to let Angie explore cooperative education as part of her high school curriculum. During her sophomore year, Angie, as part of her classwork, was a candy striper and also worked at the local hospital in housekeeping a few mornings a week. She was wonderful with the older patients. She was allowed to feed one or two of them under supervision and did so with gentle care and compassion.

Angie, however, did have a bit of impishness that made me want to check on her from time to time. Because she was cute and sweet, she occasionally got away with things that she should not have. One day I went to check on her and found her sitting with her feet up and drinking a Coke in the hospital lobby. Since she was only there a couple of hours a day, my alarm bells started ringing. I asked what she was doing. "Taking a break," she answered. I said, "Angie, you are not here long enough to take a break." She replied, "That's okay! Here Mom, let me buy you a soda!" I started to refuse, but something held me back.

I walked with her over to the soda machine. She took two coins out of her pocket and put them in the machine. I noticed they were both nickels, and the Coke machine said fifty-five cents. She whacked the vending machine a couple of times when it did not produce the soda, then said, "The darn machine took my money!" I watched her walk over to the cashier behind the lobby window and tell her that the machine had taken her Coke money and not given her a Coke. It took everything I had to keep quiet and stand back to see what happened next. The cashier gave me a funny look, pulled out a clipboard, and asked Angie to sign it to let the vendor know she had lost her Coke money. I told Angie to let me see the clipboard. She hesitated but handed it to me. There were eleven names on the sheet. Ten of them were Angie's. The cashier watched both of us with great interest. I put the clipboard down and turned to Angie, shooting her one of my "Girl, you are in serious trouble!" looks. Her eyes got big, and she stepped back, turned her face away from me, and gulped, "Oh shoot!" I dug around in my purse, handed the cashier enough money to pay for the sodas, and asked her to take Angie's names off the list. I also gave her my phone number in front of Angie and asked her to please call me if this ever happened again. The cashier said she would certainly do that.

When Angie got home that afternoon, I could tell that she was dreading her home encounter with both parents. I told Bob in front of her what had happened. We sat down with her and told her sternly that this was stealing. She would have to pay me back out of her allowance. We wrote it up on paper with the amount and made her sign it. We told her if it ever happened again the consequences would be much worse. We both hugged and kissed her, and with what sounded like great relief, she said, "I can't do *that* anymore!" And she never did. Using simple, direct communication seemed to work well with her (most of the time). Having her sign the "contract" was a concrete way to reinforce her responsibility to do better.

Angie's protective instincts sometimes got her into trouble. I received a call from Angie's high school principal during Angie's sophomore year. He asked me to come in and talk to him about a problem with Angie on the bus. One of her friends was being teased, and Angie, trying to come to her friend's rescue, used some pretty undignified language that she had heard other kids use. The kids on the bus went a little crazy laughing and yelling at the teaser, and the bus driver could not get them to calm down. This had evidently happened once before, and the driver had not told anyone but had counseled her not to do it again. Teasing on the bus was to be reported to the bus driver, not dealt with by yelling and cussing.

This time the bus driver had reported her to the principal. After the principal explained to me what had happened, he told me he was unsure what to do. I asked him what he would do if Angie did not have Down syndrome. He was obviously very uncomfortable with the whole situation. He hesitated and then told me he would call the student into his office for counseling and then give them a detention. I told him he needed to do exactly the same thing with her. He seemed very surprised, but I was adamant, and he finally agreed. I made arrangements around school to be there the day he called her into his office for her counseling. They both came out after about fifteen minutes. He had his arm around her, she was sniffling, his eyes were red, and his face was flushed. I could see that this session had been tough on both of them. I thanked him for doing the right thing and took Angie home. She completed her detention the following Saturday.

Bob and I decided early in Angie's life that this question—What would you do if Angie didn't have Down syndrome?—should be a template for how we raised her and how we approached discipline with her (with a few adjustments, of course). There are not many things sadder than a child without the benefit of loving guidance. But there is something different about the way some people look at a child with special needs and assume that guidance is lacking. I was so cognizant of this judgment as a first-time mother of a daughter with special needs, that I obsessed over everything, maybe a little too much. Were her manners appropriate? Was her hair combed and clean? Were her clothes cute enough? Will she behave properly at someone else's home without me? Etc., etc. She and Joe were well into adulthood when I realized that we have very little control over the children we are blessed with. We can only influence and try to lead by example.

We realize that every child is different, but we feel that a child should have some responsible guidance with what they learn. We tried to mete out all guidance with love and kindness. We found we could be stern and do this at the same time. We tried to use simple explanations (although at times I was humanly incapable of this), consistency of message, consistency of meaningful consequences, and simple written words. All parents struggle sometimes, but we tried to do what we deemed was right for both of our children. In spite of some of our parental missteps, both Angie and Joe turned out to be kind, caring, and independent individuals.

During her sophomore year, a young male classmate who shared several classes with Angie and who had occasionally been in trouble, smarted off to a teacher and was told to wait after class. As the other kids filed out, they teased and laughed at him. Angie, not realizing how this young man was feeling, came up behind him, leaned forward, and playfully swatted him on the shoulder. Without looking, he made a fist and swung backwards over his shoulder. If it had been anyone else, he would have hit the person in the midsection. But since Angie was short, he hit her square in the mouth, bloodying her lips. The student turned around and seemed surprised at what had happened but remained in his seat. The teacher did not see it happen, and Angie left and went on to her next class.

By the time she got to gym class, her lip was swelling and there was more blood. The PE teacher and the girls asked her what had happened. She said, "Randy punched me in the mouf, but he didn't mean to!" The PE teacher took her up to the office to get ice and get her cleaned up. Several of the kids in the class had seen the incident, and by the time school was out, everyone knew what had happened. Randy was suspended for a few days. It was probably a good thing, because word spread throughout the school quickly, and by the next day, several of the students were talking about finding him and settling the score for hitting Angie. When his suspension was up, during the first class they had together, Randy seemed embarrassed and stayed on the other side of the room. The teacher told me that Angie watched him for a while, then got up from her seat and walked over to him. "Randy," she said, "you punched me in the mouf, but I'm tougher! Now let's be friends." With that, she stuck out her hand for him to shake. It ended up being a big hug. From then on, he was her friend and protector. Whatever she needed, he made sure she had.

One of the classes that Angie loved the most was her special needs home economics class. She had a lot of fun learning basic cooking techniques and completing other life-skill projects. The teacher was putting together a unit on foreign food and culture that the kids seemed excited about. She asked me if I would mind putting together a class about Lebanese food and culture. She gave me free rein to put it together. I knew that in Angie's class there were several students from very poor rural isolated homes. School was most likely the only place they had access to a balanced meal. I also knew that other than an occasional visit to a local Mexican restaurant, most would not have opportunities to taste food from faraway places, let alone learn about different cultures.

When I asked Angie what we should make, she said, "Stuffed grape leaves!" These were her favorite, but I was afraid that they might be a little time-consuming and tedious. I decided I would make a pot of them at home and finish cooking them at school to give the students the aroma as well as the taste of this dish. This dish consists of ground beef or lamb (I used beef), rice, and spices rolled in a certain type of grape leaves and steamed with lemons and garlic in a large, covered pot. The finished products look like little green cigars and are usually served with plain yogurt. Since there was a barbecue just outside the back door of the classroom, we would make shish kabob—skewered beef cubes with cut up onions—seasoned with a mixture of cinnamon, garlic, olive oil, salt, and pepper. The students would also make my family's version of tabouli, a Middle Eastern salad with chopped parsley, cucumbers, green onions, tomatoes, and mint mixed with cracked wheat and seasoned with salt, pepper, garlic, lemon juice, and olive oil. We would have orange slices sprinkled with a little cinnamon for dessert.

As the grape leaves cooked, I had students at three different supervised stations in the kitchen area preparing what dish they had been assigned. Some were cutting up the veggies for the salad, others were putting the seasoned shish kabob and onion pieces on skewers, and others were slicing oranges and putting them on a tray to dust lightly with cinnamon. A teacher and another student were out at the grill waiting for the fire to heat up. Others rearranged tables and chairs and set out paper plates, napkins, and utensils. The room seemed to have an expectant and happy buzz. I set up a display of several of my cookbooks with beautiful pictures of the Lebanese countryside, cities, and people.

A globe with a piece of taped red yarn reaching from mid-Missouri to the country of Lebanon anchored the display, along with a map of Lebanon. At any given moment there were two or three students looking at the display and talking about what they saw. Angie proudly saw herself as an ambassador and hostess that day. She told her classmates what the food was made of and how she helped me fix it at home.

As the aroma of the grape leaves and shish kabob wafted through the school, people began stopping in. Teachers, administrators, and students alike with inquisitive expressions came in a constant stream, grabbed plates and utensils, and sampled the food. Luckily there was plenty to eat. The kids seemed so happy and proud. They ate with gusto. Later in the week, I got the most beautiful letters, one from each of the kids in Angie's class, most of them starting with "Dear Mom" (several did not have mothers at home). Many of the kids referred to me as Mom for the rest of their school time. It is one of the most moving memories I have from Angie's high school days, and it was repeated three more times. We did it each year of high school after that, and even the year after she graduated.

For a couple of hours a day during Angie's junior and Joe's freshman year, Angie worked in the lunchroom as part of a job-readiness program. She helped in the kitchen and cleared tables when other students were finished eating. As in all schools, there were always a couple of teachers there with lunchroom duty to make sure student behavior didn't get out of hand. One day, for some reason, there were no teachers in the lunchroom. Angie was clearing tables near a group of kids who had previously been in trouble for picking on other students. One of the boys, who seemed to be the ringleader, started throwing bits of food wrapping and trash at Angie. She tried to ignore him while the other boys with him laughed. He started yelling and throwing more trash at her, trying to get her to react. The kids around them, knowing what these boys were capable of, froze and watched what was happening. Angie just kept her eyes on her work. Finally, the young man got up, laughing, and walked over to her. Making sure he had the attention of the other kids, he got down to within inches of her face and started yelling. According to a witness, she hesitated, looked him in the eyes, and, loud enough for all of them to hear, told him to "F---k off!" It completely turned the tables on this bully and made him the object of laughter. Right after that happened, one of the male teachers showed up and grabbed the young man by the ear, leading him out of the lunchroom.

A student who had seen it all happen found Joe after the period ended and told him the whole story. When Joe got home that day, he came into the kitchen and said to me, "I'm going to tell you a story about something that happened at school today. It's about Angie, and you can't interrupt me till I am done. You also can't get mad at her. If you do, I will never tell you anything again, because she did exactly the right thing!" Oh, God help me, I thought. I steeled myself and listened to the story. When he finished, my first reaction was, "She said what?" My second reaction was a feeling of relief that she was okay, and then a feeling of pride. Not because she used that ugly word, but because she was able to walk away with her head held high, basically unintimidated. When she got home, I greeted her with a big hug. I waited to approach her about language, because I did not want it to seem like she was in trouble for defending herself. We waited a few days and then had a general talk about bad language and other ways to express and defend herself. She refused to talk much about the incident. We could tell it bothered her, but she always had trouble articulating her feelings when she was emotional. She preferred to take solace in comforting hugs.

Angie and Joe fought as they grew up like any other siblings. He would annoy her by going into her room, making faces at her, or poking her, or in any way that he could think of to get a rise out of her. At one point a homemade sign in Angie's handwriting appeared taped to her bedroom door that stated, "OFF LEMMONS" (off limits). Joe was never hurtful or mean, just an annoying younger brother who occasionally went too far.

One day he took her favorite purse, went into the upstairs bathroom, and locked the door. As she was pounding on the door and yelling her version of bad words (that's another story!), he flushed the toilet and told her that he had flushed her purse down the toilet. She went bananas. Angie spotted his school bookbag that had been left on the floor nearby. She picked it up, took it into the next room, and somehow got the dormer window open over the steep slanted roof of the front porch. She flung the bookbag out the window. It landed several feet down but still on the roof. We lived on busy Main Street across from the junior high school, and Joe had to climb out the window, drop down a couple of feet to the slanted roof, and gingerly walk down the shingles to get his bookbag in front of God and everyone. She had won this round, and she knew it. Joe never messed with her purse again.

They would occasionally get into a war of words on a dry erase board by the refrigerator in the kitchen. It was there for the kids or Bob to write down snacks or whatever they wanted from the grocery store. It seemed to tickle her when she could think of something really good to answer. After several notes back and forth during one exchange, she was a little agitated that she hadn't come up with anything that would make him react. She hovered around the board awhile. Then you could tell by the look on her face that she had a lightbulb moment. She grabbed the marker and wrote, "Joe needs a new dog collar and dog food. He is out." She laughed and laughed, slapping her knee, and hid in plain sight in the pantry until Joe walked into the kitchen. "Dog food!" he shrieked, feigning upset. "Dog food?" The more he shrieked, the harder she laughed. It ended with a chase around the house.

We had decided to handle things between them by observing and monitoring but not stepping in unless we felt it had gotten out of hand or someone was in danger of getting hurt physically or mentally. We honestly didn't feel we had to worry much about the relationship between them. We had gotten upstairs during the purse/bookbag fiasco in time to see Joe climbing out the dormer window and stepping sideways down the steep porch roof. The ruckus had been loud enough to hear downstairs in the kitchen where Bob and I were. We held our breaths until Joe climbed back up and in the window. We knew they were okay but her response even surprised us.

Our girl also loved high school sports! She especially loved the mascots. Whenever we were riding west on Highway 70, she would make note of the towns that we played in football, basketball, and track, and she would name all of their team mascots. One day when Grandma Louise was visiting, we decided to check out a discount shopping mall that was about an hour away. Angie was making her usual survey of the towns and their mascots when we came upon one that she could not remember. She was clearly deep in thought. She suddenly blurted out, "The Oily Thunder Frogs! That's their mascot. I made it up!" From then on, when we played this high school in any sport, we called them the Oily Thunder Frogs! Best mascot ever.

Angie's good friend Don had asked her to come to his graduation ceremony at the end of her junior year. He was a sweet young man with a ready smile, a popular football player who had a difficult home life. Somehow these two bonded, and their connection to each other was evident. They had taken solace in each other during their roughest times. He was her protector, and now Don was leaving. As was the custom at graduation, each student was given a rose. They could keep it for the memories, or they could give it to someone who had inspired them during their high school years. As the graduated students marched out after receiving their diplomas and roses, Don stopped to look for Angie in the stands. When he found her, he quickly climbed the stands, two steps at a time, to where she was sitting. He handed her his rose, and they threw their arms around each other in a tight embrace. There was not a dry eye around them. Even the principal, who had watched with concern when Don jumped out of line, cried when he saw them together.

I seriously doubted that Angie would ever go to a high school prom. I think I was just trying to avoid the disappointment of hope. Then one day, her junior year, she came home and said that a boy named Joey had asked her to prom. I was floored and called Ms. Sue, her homeroom teacher. Ms. Sue giggled and said it was true and that she would help in any way she could to make it happen. I was concerned about what Angie would wear. She was small—four feet, eight inches tall—and we often had to alter her clothes. We looked several places close to home for a dress but found nothing. There was a store in Sikeston, Missouri, where Bob's parents had moved after retirement. Grandma Louise suggested we come for a visit and shop there for her gown. Much to Grandma's delight, we found her a beautiful dress that was alterable. Our hairdresser came to the house the day of prom and did a beautiful job styling her hair, weaving in strands of tiny flowers. She looked adorable.

When Joey and his family came to pick her up, both my parents and Grandma Louise were there to witness and record this special occasion. My mother and mother-in-law were avid picture takers, so I was able to just enjoy the moment. Joe brought a moment of laughter when he re-created a scene from my high school prom by posing in the background of some of the pictures standing straight with a lampshade on his head where a floor lamp usually resided. My brother George had done the same thing during my prom pictures.

All during high school I had talked with administration about the fact that highschoolers who were in special classes were not allowed to be on the honor role. She was mainstreamed for classes like art and gym but otherwise took special education classes. We were repeatedly told that it could interfere with the class rankings of students who were going on to college. I never understood that. We tried hard to motivate Angie to a good work ethic. Her grades were good, and she loved school. We felt she and other deserving special education students should be rewarded for their efforts and achievements just as the other students were. Right before the end of her senior year, the principal called me into his office one day. He smiled and said, "I have good news! Starting next year, all special education students can be on the honor roll." I told him that made me happy, but it also made me a little sad. It had taken all of her high school years to get this accomplished, and it was too late to benefit her.

Angie graduated from high school at the age of nineteen. We were very proud of her ability to navigate the ups and downs. It was hard for us to believe that this part of her life was over. We watched her fist pump as she walked across the stage to receive her diploma and rose, and we listened to the cheers of the students and the audience as she did. We had worried about her in a smaller school with fewer services. With the guidance of some wonderful teachers and the friendship and love of fellow students, she had learned to navigate both the good and the difficult. Angie had done well. After the graduating students marched out of the auditorium and into the gathering area, she hugged us all. With a big smile, she presented her rose to Joe. He had been her rock, her very first friend in life.

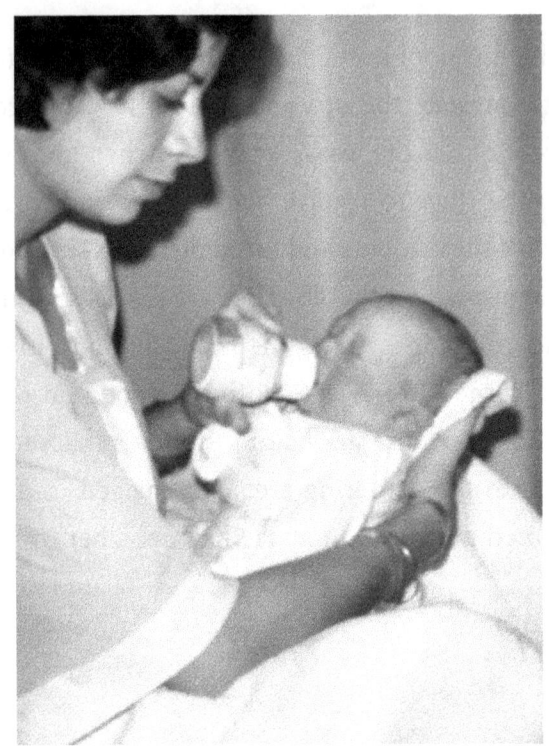

Me practicing feeding
Angela Marie
before we left the hospital

Finally home from the
hospital with Grandma
Louise and Taita Nell

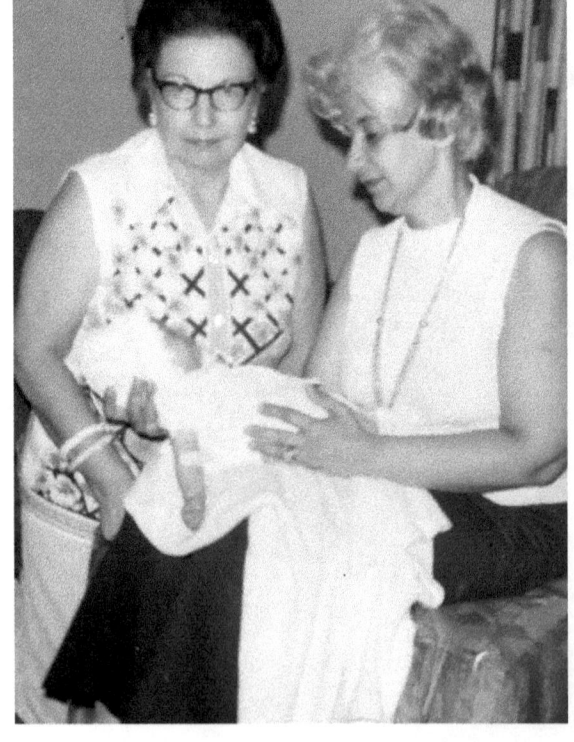

Bob's favorite picture of
Angie—in his boots!

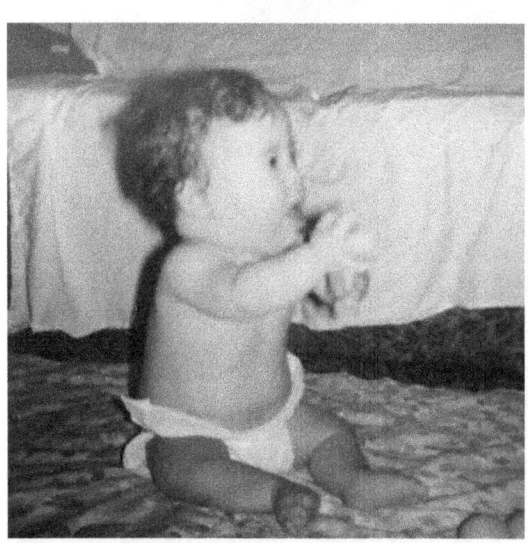

After Angie's duodenal web surgery, before her syndactyly surgery; you can see her finders that needed to be separated.

Joe, cousin Kim, and Angie

Angie examining Joe with her stethoscope

Angie and Joe with Grandma Louise and Grandpa Bob

Bob, Angie, me, and Joe

Angie and Joe with Uncle Mike (top) and Uncle George (bottom), and cousins Sarah and Michael

Angie and Joe with Father Rock for First Communion

Dad's chicken wings!
Can you tell they were Angie's favorite?

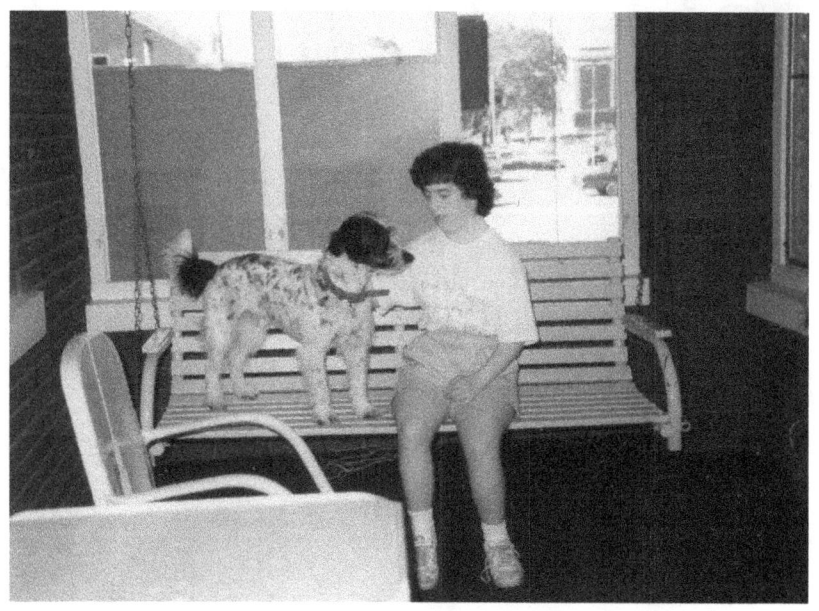

Angie with Alf on the porch

High school graduation. Can you pick Angie out of the graduates?

CHAPTER 6
ANGIE-ISMS

Angie has had a way of substituting similar-sounding words for most of her life that we find both humorous and entertaining. Joe's friend Kevin was a frequent visitor to our home during high school. Angie answered the door one day when he came over, and she asked him in. Kevin greeted her and asked for Joe. We heard her tell him Joe would be there in a minute, he was in the bathroom marinating. On another occasion when we were trying to make a point with her about something that she needed to do, she listened with teenaged resignation and answered, "Well, if you exist!" When her brother graduated from law school and she saw him in his robes, she told him he looked very extinguished. As in any sister-brother relationship, Angie at times would get so mad at Joe that she would be furious. She knew she was not supposed to use bad words, so she made up her own. The more consonants the better. Two of our made-up favorites were frikatikas and toontsio. Frikatikas could be a noun (as in, give that back, you frikatikas!) or an adjective (as in, give me my frikatikas book!). Toontsio was pretty much the same. You knew when she used those words, she was serious.

Her frequent self-talk still includes phrases to bolster her own confidence that are repeated during whatever activity she is involved in. "I am a trouper!" is one of her favorites. She used this repetitively going up and down the steps at the Cardinals ball games. "You can do this,

Angie!" is a phrase we've heard many times when she tries something new or difficult.

When asked about driving a car, she will tell us, "I can't, I'm too young!" Another phrase she used a lot when she was younger and did not want to do something was, "I can't, I'm too tall!" When she uses the word "honey" at the end of a sentence, you know she is done with whatever subject is being discussed. As in, "That's enough, honey."

She often tells me that I am "the cutest!" or "the most bee-uu-tiful mother!" Her father is a "hunk of genius!" Her brother Joe continues to be "very extinguished!" She also teases him by calling him "Roof," "Roofi," or "Rufus." We are not sure where that came from. She has used the words "hot mess" enough that her coworkers at Tiger Place presented her with a shirt with those words emblazoned on the front.

A phrase that she has often used with me when I get upset or wound up about something is, "Let it go, let it go!" She says this in a gentle voice with her hands out in front of her and her fingers in a breeze-like sweeping motion.

She also loves chicken of any kind, especially her dad's chicken wings. However, for several years, she reversed the "ch" and the "k" in both the words "chicken" and "kitchen." As in, "I am going into the chicken to get some kitchen." She loved it when I made Cornish "gay hems." She eventually outgrew the letter reversal, but we still love hearing her word substitutions. Angie has always struggled with the proper use of the words "what," "when," and "who." She basically has deferred to using "what" for all of them. We can live with that.

The difficulty she has had with articulating her feelings, especially when emotional, led us to look for ways to help her make her feelings known. A few years ago we were asked if we could be interviewed for an informational video about Woodhaven, the agency that provides community living services for Angie. After talking with her, she started crying and could not answer any questions I asked her in preparation. After she calmed down, I gave her a pencil and pad of paper with the question, "What does Woodhaven mean to you?" In list form, she wrote the following, "Independence, my peeps (her word for friends, staff, coworkers, and family), activities, work, horseback riding, my life." When asked the same question during the videotaped interview, she was able, with a smile, to list all the things she had written.

Another amazing talent that surfaced was her ability to spell any word backward that she could spell forward. We noticed this talent while she was in middle school, and it continued through high school. When asked to do this she would hesitate, look into the air intently as if seeing the word, and slowly spell it. She also memorized every license plate in our neighborhood and knew to whom the cars belonged. She reported to us every strange car that arrived, along with the plate number. We and our neighbors had our own one-girl neighborhood watch.

Special Olympics was a big part of Angie's life during high school and early adulthood. Ms. Sue and her husband, Gary, were both coaches and great advocates for athletes with special needs. Angie's participation added greatly to her physical health and wellbeing and also enabled her to feel a sense of pride and accomplishment. She brought home medals and ribbons every time she competed. She earned so many that her uncle George, an accomplished woodworker, made her a special wooden frame to hang them in. Most were gold and silver. One day after a Special Olympics sporting event out of town that we could not attend, she rushed into the house more excited than we had seen her after her previous competitions. "Look!" she yelled. "I have a bronze! Now I have all three kinds!"

CHAPTER 7
STRIVING FOR AN INDEPENDENT LIFE

Angie's insistence on her "own condo" had ramped up during her senior year. We started looking into living options for her. We found that community living with different agencies providing support was a possibility for her. Bob and I debated heavily the pros and cons of letting her go. It's what we raise our kids to do—to be independent and leave the nest. But when you have a child with special needs, it can almost take your breath away to think about this. We realized that letting her go would be better while we were still young enough to support her and oversee her living arrangements. As a geriatric nurse, one of the most difficult transitions I've seen is when the elderly parents of a person with a developmental disability are in crisis or die and the adult child is put in an unfamiliar living situation with little or no support. We also considered that if she stayed home living with us, she would never get the chance to fully mature into her version of adulthood. She would always be our child, and we would never stop acting as her parents. While she would always have oversight in a supported living situation, she would still be doing what we raise our children to do—leave home to grow into adulthood, fulfill their potential, and build a more independent life.

And so, the decision was made. She moved into a house run by a local agency with two other young ladies close to her age. Her new home was about two miles from us, but we felt like she had left the country.

We did not see her at all during the week, and we were having second thoughts. She was occupied with work at the local sheltered workshop, her roommates and friends, and her activities. She was thriving. We only saw her on Sunday when we would pick her up, take her to church, have a late lunch and, after watching her constantly check her watch for the time, take her home. After about three months of this, I finally sat her down and said, "Angie, we miss you so much; it's not the same here without you. Won't you come back to live with Mom, Dad, and Joe again?" She gently leaned over and patted my hand. "Mother," she said, "I only have time to love you on Sunday." That's when we knew that, as difficult as the decision was to let her go, we had made the right choice.

In 1994, Gary, Angie's coach, was the person in charge of the local Special Olympics. After talking with us, he submitted Angie's name and paperwork for her to be considered as an athlete for International Special Olympics. Angie had been an enthusiastic participant in regional, local, and state competitions over several years. She competed in bowling, track, basketball skills, and tennis. We happily traveled all over the state to watch her compete. For many years, Missouri State Special Olympics was held at Fort Leonard Wood, an army base in south central Missouri. The participants and chaperones slept in the barracks. We went to sleep after listening to taps. We were awakened in the early morning to the sound of reveille and our troops marching and chanting in cadence. We dined at the mess halls with the soldiers, and our trays were filled with food and treats. The soldiers went out of their way to help seat athletes and carry their food trays when needed. The army base pulled out all the stops. It was such an uplifting experience for all, including, I am convinced, the young soldiers. These young men and women in fatigues were everywhere on the grounds. They were available to help, to play frisbee, to guide participants, and to give hugs. They visited with all and pushed wheelchairs when necessary.

Opening ceremonies for the Missouri State Games during those years set the bar and mood for the rest of the week. Imagine, if you will, a parade field filled with GIs continuously stomping, chanting, and clapping in cadence. The roar was deafening, compounding the anticipatory emotions that were already building in the athletes and the spectators. It could be heard from a distance outside the stadium as the parading athletes were assembled and led in. Each group proudly carried signs representing their areas and cities. The athletes waved with great gusto, and their smiles lit the stadium. A formation of jets flying overhead caused the parade to halt, while the athletes stopped in their tracks, mouths agape. And, all of this was for them. I know that as a mother of a special needs daughter, and as a chaperone, I was not the only one who became emotional at these events. I felt emotionally overcome and in awe of the limitless possibilities that seemed to continuously present themselves because of our Angie. We understood that other experiences might have been possible if Angie had not had special needs, as they certainly were with our son, Joe. But I also realized you could say that about every child. There are different experiences and possibilities that present themselves to every child, regardless of what we think those possibilities should be. If Angie had not been a special athlete, would I have even dreamed of experiencing this amazing event? Most likely not, and I cherished every minute of it.

During the year leading up to the 1995 International Special Olympics, Angie received an invitation to a special camp for potential World Games Olympians. This camp held the final say for athlete participation in the World Games. A couple of weeks after she got home, we received a notice in the mail that Angie had been chosen as an International Special Olympian. The games would be held on Yale campus in July of 1995, and she would stay in a dorm with her team. Angie would participate as an International Special Olympian representing the state of Missouri and the USA in tennis. We were beyond thrilled. We arranged our summer schedules so that we could be there. Seven thousand athletes from almost every country in the world, their coaches, chaperones, event volunteers, and judges would be descending upon New Haven, Connecticut, for nine days. Angie and all U.S. Olympians would be flown into New Haven airport in a bevy of Lear Jets with pilot time donated from corporations and individuals all over the country. They would return home the same way.

It was a madhouse. Bob, Joe, and I went, along with my brother Mike and my mom and dad. The only lodging reservation we had been able to secure was forty miles away. When our plane arrived and we finally found our destination, there were no restaurants nearby, and we had to leave immediately for opening ceremonies. We had not been able to stop for lunch because of tight flight connections. We took a bus to the nighttime opening ceremonies and somehow made it to the stadium in time to get seated. Angie walked in with her team lead by actress Kathy Ireland, their Missouri team escort for the march. The athletes were in total awe as they marched into the Yale Bowl past the giant torch, and past Bill and Hillary Clinton and other dignitaries in the presidential boxes. After the torch lighting, a parade of famous musicians lit up the stage with performance after performance. Angie's position with her team was right next to the stage. We were worried that she would be exhausted the next day since her match was one of the first scheduled. Because of the log-jam of traffic, many of the athletes lay down on the field exhausted from the day's events until they could be bussed to their places of lodging. We were told later that presidential security added greatly to the confusion and the traffic.

The next morning, my cousin Pete, his wife Dora and their two children Loren and Michael arrived from Pine Plains, New York, to see Angie compete. He had called ahead and learned about our foodless plight. Angie was competing that morning, and he knew we had little time to stop and have a meal. He brought a couple of gallons of orange juice and a bags full of sandwiches from a restaurant along the way. I remember sitting on the concrete curb in front of the motel guzzling orange juice and eating two sandwiches. Since we had not figured out transportation to her match, we piled into Pete and Dora's oversized station wagon and hit the road. We arrived late (traffic was another story). When we got there, Angie was already on the court volleying for her tennis skills competition. She looked like a pro—her feet spread apart, knees bent, posture slightly forward, eyes focused on her opponent as she twirled her racket (she had seen some of the tennis stars do this on TV). The stands were filled with people clapping and cheering. An ESPN photographer was lying on the ground courtside, shooting up at her. Angie's poise and confidence were palpable as she completely ignored the photographer and the commotion, concentrating on her volley. Bob became emotional and burst into tears. How do you explain the feelings you experience seeing your child in this scenario when you've been through complicated diagnoses, hospitalizations, life-threatening surgeries, and sometimes the pitying looks of strangers?

Angie took the Olympic silver medal that day. She was the first medalist for the state of Missouri at the International Special Olympics in 1995. During her participation, Angie volleyed with Monica Seles and her father, the Jensen brothers, and various professional athletes. She rubbed elbows with famous people like Tracy Austin, Miss America, Arnold Schwarzenegger, and members of the Kennedy family. I was struck by how the Kennedy family, the stars, and the professional athletes milled around and through the crowds. No entourages, no bodyguards.

Just open and approachable people with ready eye contact and smiles. We laughed heartily when one of our Missouri Special Olympians remarked after an encounter with Eunice Shriver, who was wearing a top and slacks that did not match, "Eunice needs the fashion police!"

When we returned home, we saw that our town paper had run an article about Angie being a medalist, along with write-ups about the successes of the rest of our mid-Missouri team. Even though Angie was in supported living, we thought she should stay with us a few days after she came home, just to decompress. It had been a wonderful but emotionally charged experience for her. I stayed home with her for a few days. We talked, we hugged, she expressed feelings, and she cried as we both recharged. They were happy emotional tears. Toward the end of the few days, I asked her one more time how she was feeling. Angie looked at me, smiled, and said with confidence, "I am a famous star and a heavy dude!" I think this experience had a profound effect on all of us.

Another natural occurrence of her age and stage was her escalating interest in male companionship. Angie really wanted a boyfriend. "Mom, you need to help me find a boyfriend!" was a common beginning for conversations between the two of us. As she developed crushes on different coworkers and friends, we started wondering about intimacy. Angie was a charming but innocent flirt. We had seen her in action and knew that her crushes were not always on individuals who were appropriate for a young woman with a cognitive disability. The possibility of her being taken advantage of was frightening to us. Women with Down syndrome can become pregnant. We worried a lot about this. We felt a pregnancy would be not only traumatic but dangerous for her. Her understanding of what could cause a pregnancy was indeed fuzzy.

A pregnancy with her heart anomalies could be a disaster, let alone giving birth, and that of course was only one of many concerns we had. There were many conversations with her about not letting anyone touch her body. She had the power to say no!

We thought long and hard about how to proceed and finally made an appointment with her doctor. He had known Angie for a few years and was as concerned as we were. We discussed several options. Angie was over eighteen and her own guardian. We consulted an attorney friend to understand our rights as parents in the decision-making process, as well as her rights as an individual. Birth control pills seemed to be her best option, and Angie started on them soon after. The realization that there was very little we could control was at times like a slap in the face. We found this to be true with both Angie and Joe, as it is with all children. All that any parent can ever do is be vigilant and try to prepare their children for safety to the best of their ability.

CHAPTER 8
MOVE TO WOODHAVEN

Angie had been in supported living for two years, and we decided there might be more opportunities for activity and employment for her in a nearby larger town. I worked in Columbia, Missouri, for a continuing care community. There was an organization serving people with special needs that was affiliated with the continuing care community where I worked. I loved the mission and values it expressed. Woodhaven had been established in 1964 caring for people with differing abilities. It was no longer a campus-based organization. They had moved a majority of the people served out into the greater community so they would be better enabled to fully participate in the life of the community at large.

Angie moved to Woodhaven in 1995, the year Joe graduated from high school. Joe had investigated many colleges and seemed to keep coming back to St. Louis University as one of his top choices. One of the things required of a prospective student was an essay on the person who has influenced them most during their life. Joe wrote a beautiful essay about Angie. We were so taken with this gesture of love for his sister. We mentioned it to a friend who was doing some public relations for a politician who had championed the rights of special needs individuals and was running for reelection. Joe's essay was referenced and quoted in a speech this politician made. Joe was accepted to St. Louis University and left home a few months before Angie moved away. We were suddenly empty nesters and felt the emptiness and the excitement that comes with that stage of life.

After her move, Angie hit the ground like a track star and never looked back. Woodhaven embraced her. Almost immediately, she fell in love with her roommates and staff and her home coordinator, Sandra. Her housemate was Mendy, and Peggy and Meredith lived next door. Their home was a duplex in a desired part of town, with each lady having their own room and Woodhaven maintaining an office and a bedroom for overnight staff on Peggy and Meredith's side. It worked well. Angie felt connected but independent at the same time. It was decided that she could spend up to two hours at any one time at home without supervision. She relished this time alone. She was fully assessed for likes, dislikes, favorite activities, routines, needs, and habits. They asked and honored her opinion on all matters of her life. When she came home on Sundays, she made us laugh with tales of her life and her roommates' lives. She beamed as she told us about her activities. She loved her wonderful staff and her new life. They treated her and her roommates more like friends than clients. I would hear about shopping trips, movies, dinners out, Mizzou sporting events, and regular trips to see Julie, her hairdresser—the things we all enjoy.

One Sunday Angie was talking in a very animated fashion about a new friend she had made. We were trying to place this person since we had met many of the Woodhaven clients and staff. We asked descriptive questions about things like height, hair color, size without narrowing the field. I finally asked Angie if this new friend was black or white. Angie looked at us thoughtfully for a moment and then said, "No... She's pink and has a nice smile!"

Bob and I looked at each other, both of us realizing that Angie's approach to people included nothing having to do with exterior descriptors. It was only what was on the inside that counted to her.

On rare occasions, Angie would become upset with a staff member. There are no perfect organizations, but in twenty-seven years of Angie getting services from Woodhaven, I can only think of one instance that I felt was serious. It was shortly after she had gone to live there. A new staff member dropped Angie and Mendy off at Walmart and left them there for two hours while she went shopping elsewhere. Angie was understandably livid! It was frightening and exhausting. Both supervisory staff and Angie called to tell us about the incident soon after they got home. I was ready to bring her back home, but she resisted. She wanted to stay where she was.

The staff member was placed on immediate leave, and Woodhaven quickly called a meeting to review the incident and decide what to do about the staff member. The meeting included Angie, Mendy, and me, as well as supervisory and executive staff. Angie and Mendy were asked what they wanted to have happen. Angie stated that she did not want that person in her home anymore. Mendy concurred. Woodhaven honored their wishes, and the staff member was let go. It helped Angie and Mendy understand that they both had power over their environment and their lives. It helped me understand what was at the heart of Woodhaven's mission—empowering and enabling the lives of the people served. A good question to ask when considering supported living is: Are the people served empowered to make decisions within their abilities? As a geriatric nurse, I know that even the most physically and cognitively dependent individuals have ways of expressing their wants and needs, likes and dislikes. If only we are willing to listen in whatever way it takes for us to hear.

Angie adored her cousins, although none lived close by. Both Angie and Joe relished the time they spent with their cousins during holidays and vacation visits. My brother George had moved to Idaho for work. His first wife, Marty (mother of cousins Michael and Sarah), sadly had passed away when the kids were very young. He later married Renee, thus adding Megan to the cousin list. We all loved it when they came for visits. Most often, we saw Bob's brother Jim and his wife, Kay, and their kids, Kim and Jay, who lived in south Missouri. Kim was less than a year younger than Joe, and Jay was ten years younger. During early family gatherings, they all had fun together putting on skits to entertain us.

Bob's parents, Angie and Joe's beloved grandparents, both died in 1998—his mother unexpectedly on July fourth, his dad, the following Christmas night. Bob Sr. had gone into a veterans' home in 1994 in Cape Girardeau, Missouri, after his Alzheimer's had progressed beyond Louise's ability to care for him at home. She had done her best, but it had taken a toll on her health. They had celebrated their fiftieth anniversary with a big party just days before he went into the home. The next morning, in a heartbreaking exchange between the two of them, he asked her what all those "things" (anniversary gifts) were sitting on their dining room table. He had no memory of their previous day's celebration. She had told us many times that she could not bear to bury her husband, and she did not have to.

One sweet memory we have demonstrates their love after fifty plus years of marriage. Bob Sr., because of the armed forces décor in the veterans' home, thought he resided there because he was in service. During one visit when we were all together, he grinned, leaned over to Louise, and said, "If I can ever get out of here on pass, I'm gonna come take you on a date!"

The funerals were difficult for the family but especially for Angie. Both were great tributes, but Bob Sr.'s was especially meaningful, with a wonderful minister who took the time to meet with the grandchildren and listen to their grandma and grandpa stories. She included in her sermon Angie's thoughts of them RV camping and eating ice cream in heaven.

Some time later, Cousin Kim and her fiancé, Matt, announced their wedding plans for the summer of 2000. She called me one afternoon and said she really wanted Angie to be in her wedding. She had already talked with Joe and asked him to be part of the wedding party. The wedding would take place outside on a beautiful grassy point overlooking Table Rock Lake.

The bridesmaid dresses were a beautiful pale blue. Kim was insistent that Angie participate in all the bridal party festivities occurring a few days before the wedding. Angie had a blast with all the bridesmaids and enjoyed getting her hair done, watching everyone get made up (she still absolutely refuses to wear any makeup!), participating in the banter, and acting like the mother hen, at times cautioning the bridesmaids to behave.

Angie would be given a basket of beautiful long-stemmed single flowers to carry as she was escorted to the wedding arch. The plan was that during the ceremony, members of both families, including Joe, would each take one flower from her basket and place it in a vase. This co-mingling of single flowers of all different sizes and shapes to make one beautiful bouquet would signify the uniting of the two families. When the time came, Angie decided to take charge of the flowers and the flower distribution. She watched each person thoughtfully as they came to her. She then gently rifled through the flowers, carefully selecting and handing them what she chose as the exact perfect flower to represent their contribution to the unity vase. It probably took a little longer than was planned, but no one seemed to mind.

I Only Have Time to Love You on Sunday

CHAPTER 9
MEANINGFUL WORK AND A HAPPY LIFE

Once she was settled at Woodhaven, Angie knew she wanted to find a job. She had worked in a sheltered workshop since she graduated, but Woodhaven felt she was capable of a job out in the community. Woodhaven set up interviews for her with three different job coaching agencies. She was adamant about the one she wanted. We asked her how she came to her decision. She told us she chose the one who talked to her instead of talking to the staff who accompanied her. Her assessment found that she liked to clean. She went through several jobs that were just not good fits. One expected her to get down on her knees and scrub floors in the bathroom. She had trouble reaching behind the toilets. That didn't last. Another was interrupted when the place where she worked came under new management and she was fired without her job coach present. It was heartbreaking, but she recovered and survived.

Another job she had that she loved was for a contracted food service in one of the large cafeterias on a local college campus. Joe was in law school on campus for part of that time, and she loved seeing him there occasionally. She called the kids "my college students." She bussed and cleaned tables and emptied trash. She worked with great people who coached her and helped her establish a consistent work pattern. After she had been there about three years, the company who had the dining contract cut back on staff. Angie's job was not cut, but her immediate supervisor, who had been so helpful to her, was let go.

Her boss was now an assistant manager of food service. He would come out of his office and bark at her to drop what she was doing and start something else. If she eventually completed what he told her to do, it would not be until after she finished the task she had first started. Her work pattern was established, and it was really confusing and hard for her to change directions. His perceived attitude and stern tone of voice did not help. After it happened a few times, he somehow took this ingrained pattern to mean deliberate insubordination of his directions. Her job coach tried explaining better ways to communicate with Angie to the manager, then explained to Angie better ways to adjust to his direction, but, like Angie, the manager just did not understand.

Angie internalized the tension, and you could tell she was becoming anxious during her off-work hours. Her Woodhaven staff tried to help her talk about it, but Angie's difficulty in articulating her feelings when emotional continued to surface. The last time he came out to tell her to do something different in his stern tone of voice, she told him forcefully she couldn't do that, she had to take care of the trash first. He fired her and sent an email around to every cafeteria on campus saying that she could not be rehired. We all cried for a couple of days. It was devastating to see her so misunderstood and disrespected. We realized we probably should have taken her out of that job sooner, but she loved "her college students."

After the cafeteria fiasco, Angie went back to the workshop for a while. She regrouped, relaxed in the environment, and regained her self-confidence. With the passing of time, the job coaching agency ACT contacted us and said they felt she was ready to try working in the community again. She really wanted to clean and embarked on a series of smaller temporary cleaning jobs, developing skills and working on habits.

We had an opportunity to meet some of Bob's relatives—Mary, John, and their daughter Martha—at a beach condo in San Diego for a short vacation right after Christmas 2002. It was a great getaway, but the plane ride home took a very scary turn. Angie went into an episode of tachycardia. She was stable, joking with her brother, but I could see her heart pounding through her shirt. Since the plane was close to landing, we alerted the flight attendant and arranged to have an ambulance meet our plane in Kansas City. It was late at night, and the ambulance took us to the closest hospital. The emergency room diagnosis was supraventricular tachycardia. She was given an IV and put on a medical drip to stop the abnormal rhythm. It took several minutes, but it finally worked. They kept her until about 4 a.m. for observation. We were told if it happened again when we got her home, to call an ambulance to get her to the hospital immediately.

We had an exhausting two-hour drive home. We decided to keep her with us for a couple of days to make sure everything was okay. She was fine the next morning, but I decided she needed to stay with us one more night. The second morning I could hear her in the shower and noticed she had made her bed. She came out of her room fully dressed and said calmly, "Mom, my heart is beating fast again." We called the ambulance. It was there in a matter of minutes, and I rode with her to the hospital about twenty minutes away. She was completely calm, talking to and smiling at the paramedics.

When we arrived, the ER staff swung into action, wheeling her gurney immediately into a room and starting an exam, ordering fluids and giving orders with people in and out of the room. Angie looked up wide-eyed and exclaimed, "Wowwwee, just like *ER*, ten, nine central, Saturday night!" This time her medication drip did not work; she stayed in tachycardia, and they ended up giving her a second IV dose. That did the trick. Again, they kept her for observation for several hours. As we sat there with her, exhausted and worried, staff came in and out to check on her. One male nurse started teasing her. It was all good-natured, but after several comments back and forth I could tell she was getting tired of the exchange. She turned and asked Bob when Joe would be there. The nurse asked, "Is Joe your brother?" Angie said, "No, he's my lawyer!" Brother Joe was in his last year of law school. The nurse started laughing and said he'd better back off with the teasing.

On the drive home, we decided to have Angie stay with us at least one more night. She seemed fine the rest of the day. However, the next morning I went in to check on her and found her making her bed. I asked how she was feeling. "My heart's beating fast again," she said. We immediately called the ambulance again. Luckily, it was the same two paramedics. They remembered her and called the hospital on the way in. The doctors could not get the abnormal rhythm stopped and did a cardioversion. It didn't work the first time, and they repeated it with no success. We were beside ourselves. We were so afraid we would lose her! They admitted her to the cardiac intensive care unit. She was immediately put on a stronger medication in drip form. She did not want me to leave, and I ended up staying the night with her. The nurses were efficient and reassuring. There were frequent assessments, and the drip finally relieved her tachycardia. There was one very young nurse working nights. He came into the room a few minutes after midnight and started taking her vitals. It woke her up. He told her that since she was awake, he needed to ask her some questions. What's your name, what city do you live in, where are you, what's the date? She answered all correctly until his last question. I could tell she was exasperated by being awakened and having to answer. "What day is it?" he repeated. With emphasis, she answered, "It's tomorrow, honey!" With that, she turned her back to the nurse and went back to sleep. There were no more questions posed.

Angie ended up having a procedure called an ablation before she came home from the hospital. Dr. Dan was a calm, sweet man whom we also knew from church. As we walked back to the entrance of the surgical suite with her on the gurney, she got up on one elbow, looked us both in the eye, and said, "Don't worry about me, I'll be just fine!" And she was. She recovered as if nothing had happened. The day she came home, she picked up where she had left off and was ready to reengage in all her activities. We tried to slow her down a little but finally just let go and sent her back home to her friends.

As Angie's thirtieth birthday approached, we started talking about what we could do to celebrate. She had been part of the Woodhaven family and part of her Newman Center Church family for nine years. After much discussion, the following came to us: she would most likely not get married, so this party needed to be as much of a celebration as a wedding reception would be. We would make it a memorable life event! We contacted a local caterer whose son had been one of Angie's friends in high school, and we secured the large upstairs reception hall at the Newman Center for a Saturday night close to her birthday. A very talented friend made the most gorgeous cake. A local DJ who had played for a Special Olympics event was contacted and agreed to play. We decided it needed to be a surprise party. The invitations were sent, and we ended up with 125 people attending! It was a party to end all parties! When Angie's staff members brought her into the room and all assembled yelled, "Surprise!" she looked stunned, recovered immediately, and went person to person, hugging, shaking hands, and working the room.

The party was an astounding event attended by her Woodhaven "peeps," her church family, many of our relatives, school friends, and neighbors. Until that party, we never knew how well Angie could line dance; she certainly showed me up. Dancing continued through the evening. Her uncle Jim videotaped the event, and it was so much fun to rewatch everything. Our pastor, Father Charlie, came to the party and later told us how wonderful he thought it was that we had created this life event for her. The next morning at mass, he asked Angie to stand. He told the congregation about the party and what a meaningful celebration it was. He then led the parishioners in a standing ovation for her.

Joe graduated from law school later that year. Angie was so proud of her brother's accomplishment. Her only sadness was that he would move back to St. Louis, where he still lives and works.

In May of 2005, three months after Mom and Dad had moved from St. Louis into independent living at Tiger Place in Columbia, Missouri, my mother, Nell, passed away. Tiger Place was a joint effort between the School of Nursing and the School of Engineering at the University of Missouri, in partnership with the Americare Corporation. Its purpose was to research care and technology that will help people stay in their homes longer. It is considered independent living but is also licensed as intermediate care so that needed help could be brought to people as they aged. We felt it was the perfect place that would allow them to be together in a safe environment where Dad would have help. Dad was very reluctant, but Mom was relieved to make the move.

The end came more quickly than any of us had anticipated. Mom had been worried about my dad, in her words, "rattling around the house (in St. Louis) alone" after she died. Mom's death was not unexpected; she had been ill for a while. She had been put on hospice shortly after they moved. I remember her asking Dr. Clay exactly what hospice meant. He was honest, direct, but kind, telling her it meant that she probably had six months or less to live. She furrowed her brow, counted the months on her fingers, then exclaimed, "Darn! I really wanted to go to that wedding!" She was at Tiger Place long enough to make a strong impression on both staff and her fellow residents. Her sustained humor and her positive attitude, even in the throes of a terrible disease process, made everyone smile. Angie as usual stayed on the periphery, refusing to attend the funeral. She came to the burial releasing white balloons that seemed to hover over her for a few seconds before taking off. The star that Angie picked for Taita was the brightest one in the sky.

After Mom died, my dad was surrounded by his new friends, the residents, and staff. More importantly, her essence was present in his apartment and throughout the building. He acknowledged that it would have been different if he had moved there after her death.

In 2009, Angie had been looking for a job for a while. ACT had called Tiger Place, along with several other possible places of employment, but had yet to receive an answer back. I happened to mention to the executive director at that time, Brian, that ACT had called. He immediately gave me his cell phone number and asked that they call it instead of the general number. After deciding on a list of possible duties, Angie went in for an interview. She was nervous and excited to start. In light of past experiences, we impressed upon her how important it was that she listen to her supervisor, communicate with her job coaches, and stay focused on her work. It was difficult at first, but after a few glitches, she seemed to settle in. She saw her grandfather (Jiddo) every day! Dad used to joke that she was a spy hired to keep an eye on him. After a quick hug, she would get right back to work. She worked keeping the common areas and halls clean, vacuuming and dusting and cleaning bathrooms. She and her supervisors maintained a checklist of duties for her that could change from day to day. As long as she could see it on paper, she could follow it. Checking the list became part of her routine.

The residents loved seeing her and would tell Dad how much they loved watching her go about her duties. As she became more familiar with her duties, she greeted residents by name. For the first time, she felt part of something that appreciated her. Of course, there were slip-ups, but they were corrected in a manner that she could understand and follow. I worried every time a new executive director showed up or a new housekeeping supervisor was hired. My worries were unfounded. She was always treated with kindness and respect while being held accountable for her duties. Many of the residents became like grandparents to Angie. It was common for Dad to hear from his neighbors about what a good job she was doing. She loved them too and took great pride in being part of the staff who cared for "her" residents.

When Angie was approaching her fortieth birthday, we decided we needed to plan another celebration. We asked what she wanted—a party, a trip? She chose a party. We asked what kind of party she wanted and where she wanted to have it. Without hesitation, she said she wanted "a bash at Tiger Place with my Tiger Place peeps and my Woodhaven peeps!" We wondered what that would be like, if there would be some disconnection between the two groups, and how we would keep everyone entertained. Joe made the suggestion that we should have karaoke. Bob and I just looked at each other. Karaoke? How would that work for these two separate groups? Not being able to come up with any other options, we decided to go with it. We found a young lady who volunteered to come with her karaoke setup and MC the party. Angie and Joe's uncle Jim and aunt Kay and her cousin Olivia also came, along with other family and friends. Since Angie was an employee of Tiger Place, she could not accept gifts from her Tiger Place peeps. Angie asked if she could have a box to collect donations for Woodhaven if anyone wanted to give. Her executive director allowed it.

As the party commenced, it was a little awkward at first, but then the karaoke started. Olivia and our young bonus grandchildren Ellie and Thomas (who had asked us to be their grandparents) got up to sing several songs together. One of the staff members came forward and said that if we put on "Boogie Woogie Bugle Boy," one of the residents, John, would start dancing. We put it on, and he did not disappoint! He solo-danced his heart out, kicking and skipping to cheering and clapping. The smiles and laughter all around told us there was no disconnect here; both groups were enjoying themselves and each other. The singing never really died down. At one point, I was hip/arm-checked out of the way by Angie's housemate, Lucy, who had dragged me up to sing with her because she was feeling shy. She got about halfway through the song when her confidence exploded, and she threw her arms wide open, sending me into the wall. She never missed a lick and finished the song by herself. When it was time for the party to be over, no one left. The residents stayed and continued to visit with remaining Woodhaven clients, staff members, and family. Angie's box for Woodhaven collected almost three hundred dollars in donations.

Angie had a wonderful life at Woodhaven. It was filled with activities, friends, volunteering, dances, potlucks, and lots of laughter. Her roommates and another Woodhaven resident, Jeff, who lived in an apartment across the lane, all became a group and hung out together. When they went anywhere, they went as a group. Angie and Jeff had always been good friends, and in time, they became an item. You could tell he was smitten. He was always at her elbow. They were adorable together. Angie knew she had the upper hand in this relationship, and their antics together brought lots of smiles and laughter to those who surrounded them. Angie called him "Jeffy-Poo" and would let out a little giggle when she said it. He would call her "sweetheart." She also had her eye-roll down as if they'd been married for thirty years. When she got exasperated at Jeff for eating too many cookies or drinking soda (he was diabetic), she would tell me she needed a boyfriend without glasses! We were never sure what that meant, but her exasperation never lasted long. For her birthday one year he bought her a ring. You could tell he wanted her to put it on her ring finger. She loved the ring and wore it faithfully, but she would only wear it on her first finger. If he said anything, she would lean into him, giggle, and say, "Now, Jeffy-Poo!" They would smile sweetly at each other, and that would be the end of that!

We attended the Newman Center Church every Sunday. Angie loved the choir, and she always chose the seats right next to them. She would joyfully clap, sing, and dance when the choir played. Everyone in the choir knew her, and some would bring her their envelopes to put in the collection basket for them. After mass was over, we could not leave until she got her own church bulletin. She would take it home and read it cover to cover, often asking me what different words meant. One Sunday while reading, she asked me what a "yowth" was. I asked her to spell the word. "Y-O-U-T-H," she replied. "Oh, youth!" I said. "That is a child or young person." Her eyes lit up. "I am a youth!" she said excitedly. "I want to sing in the youth choir! I have a very bee-uu-tee-ful voice!" Unfortunately, Angie takes after both of her parents. Neither of us can carry a tune. My heart sunk wondering what I could possibly say to this. Then, I was hit by a bolt of divine intervention: "And that's why God wants you to lead the singing in the pews!" Angie snapped a finger on each hand and pointed at me. "Yes!" she said. "I have to lead the singing in the pews!" I breathed a sigh of great relief.

We ended up moving from our seats by the choir to the back of the church when my dad was still attending mass with us and no longer could get in and out of the pew very easily. The chairs against the wall had arms and were more comfortable for him. It was also an easier walk for him in and out of the church. After Dad was no longer able to come to church, we still sat back there on occasion.

Angie's heart had seemed to be doing well for several years after our crazy plane ride back from our vacation in San Diego, but one Sunday at mass, Angie told me her chest was "jumping up and down." I could tell she was frightened. I was too (this had recently happened twice before). At the time she told me, one of her cardiologists, Dr. Dan, was singing a solo in our church choir. I left her in her seat with a friend closely watching her, and walked around the large church to Melissa, the choir director's wife (another friend). I asked her to have Dr. Dan come and see us in the back when he was done. He came immediately after, took her pulse, talked with her, walked us out to the car, and told us to go to the emergency room. We sat in the waiting room for a while, but we finally got a room, and Angie was hooked up to an EKG.

Our parish priest, Father Rich, heard about Angie. He showed up and sat with us in the emergency room for a while. He could tell I was a little stressed. He said a short prayer with us, then joked with Angie about behaving before he left. An appointment was made with her other long-time cardiologist, Dr. John, who talked to us about inserting a loop recorder. The recorder was a small, very thin capsule about an inch long, just under the skin over her heart, that would record her normal rhythm and rate over time and send any significant abnormalities via internet back to her physicians. We had planned to leave on our yearly family reunion vacation to Cooperstown, New York, a week later. With her complex medical history, we were really concerned about taking her out of state and having something happen again while she was away from her regular doctors. Since being in supported living, Angie had Medicaid insurance and SSI. That meant that if something happened in New York, an appeal would have to be made to Missouri Medicare for payment to be made for out-of-state care. That worried us too.

Dr. Dan suggested the loop recorder capsule be implanted before we left. He offered us an appointment to get it implanted in just a few days. It was a very brief procedure, and there would be no down time for recovery after. We grabbed the chance. At least this way if something did happen, we would have data input about the cause and advice from her physicians before heading home.

We arrived a little early at the hospital clinic on the day it was to be implanted. Sandra, Angie's beloved home coordinator of many years, came. She was like a second mother to Angie, someone she loved and trusted. It was great to have her there. Angie was called back and prepped, and I was allowed to come back to wait with her until Dr. Dan got there. This was not his normal clinic day, and he had been delayed by an emergency. She laughed and joked with everyone while she waited, but suddenly her whole demeanor changed. Sandra, Bob, and I could not tell what had happened. She became very frightened and would not lie down. Her eyes were glazed; her breathing was increased and shallow.

She would not let go of my arm. I tried to reason with her, but it seemed that she could not hear me. I worried it was some kind of a seizure, so I pinched her arm lightly. Angie reacted. It was a panic attack.

I really thought she would calm down when Dr. Dan got there. She adored him. He tried talking to her, but again there was no response. She was in such a state that he gave her some medication to calm her. It did absolutely nothing. Her vitals were monitored throughout this episode. Although her usually low heart rate was up, her rhythm was unchanged. He calmly told us we would just have to revisit the loop recorder another time and then sat down at the desk in the middle of the room to write his notes. Angie told us she had to go to the bathroom. She got off the table with our help, walked behind Dr. Dan on her way, balled up her fist, slugged him square between the shoulder blades, and kept walking. We were stunned. Dr. Dan turned around and asked Angie in a calm voice if that was a love pat. She didn't answer. Sandra said she would help her get dressed, so I left to go tell Bob, who was in the waiting room, what had happened. His first words back to me were a reminder not to yell at her. I knew if I did, I would put her on the defensive, and she would never be able to tell us what she was feeling.

I apologized to Dr. Dan. He was so calm! He told me he was not mad or upset, that it was probably just too much too soon for her. When he said that, I realized that a decision had been made without her input. In the past, unless it was something extremely urgent, we had prepped her well for things, allowing her to digest and distill any information before proceeding. We really had not included her in the decision. I wanted so badly to talk with her, but I did not. She went home. I got a call from Dr. Dan's nurse the next day. His message was to go ahead with our vacation plans for the following Monday. He felt if her cardiac rhythm had remained stable enough throughout her episode, he was sure she would be fine. He said to call him or Dr. John if we needed them while we were gone.

The following Sunday, I picked Angie up for 11 a.m. mass. She seemed over the trauma and on to other things. In the car during a lull in the conversation, I told her I had a question for her. "Angie," I started, "do you want Dr. Dan to still be your doctor, because I don't think he knows that you do." She did not answer me. When we got to church, she got out of the car and took off, not waiting for me. When I got into the building, I did not see her anywhere. I went to the back of the church to our usual seats and sat down, still looking for her. I then spotted Angie and Dr. Dan coming out of the choir room behind the altar with their arms around each other, both smiling. I almost cried as they parted, Angie coming to sit with me, and Dr. Dan going up to the choir platform. I don't know exactly what was said that day, and I never asked, but I am betting there was an apology offered and forgiveness returned.

Another message for me here is that sometimes you just don't know what the right thing to do is. It's hard to figure out the reasons for some of Angie's behaviors, because to us the behavior doesn't always fit the need that is being expressed. You just have to keep digging to find out.

A few months later, Angie brought me a picture she had drawn on a small piece of paper. It was a picture of a stick figure lying on a gurney with a stunningly accurate depiction of the layout of the clinic room she had occupied during her previous attempt to get the loop recorder placed. The monitor that recorded vitals was on the left, with the blood pressure cuff on the figure's stick arm, the pulse oxygenation clip on its finger. There were leads from the figure's chest to an EKG machine. On the other side was the monitor that the loop recorder, once placed, would send signals to. On the stick figure's chest lay the loop recorder, depicted many times its normal size. After I had looked the drawing over for a few seconds, Angie said, "That's me. I am ready; I need to get the loop recorder for my heart." I asked if she was sure. She said yes. I noted the picture and told her the loop recorder was very tiny, not like what she had drawn. She said she knew. I asked if she wanted me to call Dr. Dan. She said yes.

Dr. Dan met with Angie and me. After she assured him she was ready, he said he would be happy to place the loop recorder for her. He told us that they were doing the procedure in a prepared clinic room in their office suite now, not in the hospital clinic. It would be much quieter with less busy confusion. The loop recorder was placed a few days later without any problems. It took only a few minutes from the time we got there until it was done. The loop recorder lasted four years. For most of that time, her cardiac rhythm was transmitted monthly along with any concern that we had. We carried the transmitter with us to New York and for any overnight away during that four-year period. When it came time to replace it, Dr. Dan and Dr. John both felt that it was unnecessary. Her heart rate remained irregularly regular, if that makes sense. Although her heart rate remains slow, and her rhythm is irregular, she is not symptomatic in her daily life and activities.

I spent my early years in a little town about thirty miles north of Cooperstown, New York, called Fort Plain. There is a large Hage (my maiden name) family reunion there yearly. My cousins and their children have shown up at the state park on beautiful Otsego Lake the first Sunday in August every year without reminder since the 1960s. The original family reunion started long before in the backyard of my aunt Vicky's house. It's a loud, happy, and loving gathering that Angie always looks forward to. After my mom passed away in 2005, we took a trip to the family reunion for the first time in eleven years. Most of my cousins had come for Mom's funeral, and I felt such a longing to reconnect with them! We all had been busy raising families and with life in general. My family had moved away when I was nine years old. I had always missed my cousins, my first friends and playmates, but seeing them at my mom's funeral had intensified the longing in my heart to reconnect with them. While we were there in Cooperstown, we started looking at and admiring the old homes in this beautiful and historic little town. Bob, who had always had an interest in real estate, decided to look at a couple of local homes that might be for sale. I thought he was nuts but was curious to see what was available. I went along with it only for that reason, knowing he would not buy anything. After all, we lived in Missouri, and this was New York, 1,200 miles away. My cousin Chuck hooked us up with a local real estate agent, Donna, and we started to look around.

The first house we looked at that day somehow remained in our thoughts all day long. Everything else we saw was a comparison. It was one of the newer homes in town, built in 1911. It had a perfect large front porch and four bedrooms upstairs. It was solid and had been very well cared for. It had a small but private backyard and a good-sized two-story carriage barn at the end of a long driveway. It was decorated in 1970s style by the lovely older couple who had owned it for the last fifty years. They were going into an assisted living apartment, and we could tell they wanted someone to buy it who loved it as much as they did. The 1970s wallpaper and paneling somehow added to the quirkiness of the house. We made an offer the next day and signed the papers before we went home. I remember thinking on the way back to Missouri that we must have been crazy to do what we did. At that point, we did not realize that this house would become a gathering place for family and a huge blessing in our lives for the next fourteen years.

Angie loved going to Cooperstown and seeing the family at the yearly August reunions. My cousins and their adult kids and families became a big part of her family. She glowed with all the attention. It was amazing to us how she remembered all of their names from year to year.

Bob and I started visiting Cooperstown several times a year. Because she was working, Angie only went once a year. She had her own room in the house, as did my dad as long as he was able to go with us. The family loved having Dad, now the patriarch of the family, come to visit, and they surrounded him with love and respect. When we were alone at the house, he and Angie would sit on the front porch for hours playing checkers, greeting passersby, and basking in the beautiful summer breezes.

We started a tradition of having a party at the house the night before the big family reunion for all who could attend. One of my cousin's sons had become a Catholic priest. Since the reunion was held on Sunday, Father Jason sometimes said mass for the family the afternoon before at our home in our long narrow living room. It was such a special intimate service with dozens of people in attendance. After mass, the dinner buffet would open up and the party would commence, lasting long into the evening. It would spill out onto the front porch and into the backyard, the carriage barn, and the length of the driveway. I never was burdened with worrying about cleanup, because the whole family pitched in.

We sold the house in 2019. The realization had set in that Bob and I were getting older, and the distance we traveled to get there was getting more difficult for us. Upkeep was also going to be a challenge in the future as our handyman was talking about moving. We continue to go back for the Hage family reunion every year. It's become Angie's annual "vee-cation."

I was helping Angie prepare for one reunion trip to Cooperstown when she left the bedroom to talk with her roommates. I stayed in the room to finish her packing. Jeff immediately came in. "Mrs. Minner," he said, "I need your help." "Okay, Jeff, what do you need?" I asked.

He said, "You need to help Angie buy me a present!" "A present?" I repeated. He said, "Yes! I am her man, and she should buy me a present because I will miss her very much!" I said, "Okay, Jeff, I will see what I can do." Angie loved to shop in Cooperstown and usually spent money on a new purse, wallet, or something for herself, but not much else. During this trip, whenever I mentioned Jeff wanting a present, she told me she had already given him one before she left. We went to our usual shops in Cooperstown. She found herself a new travel bag that took all her money. This did not look good for Jeff. I really felt bad, so I ended up picking up a small souvenir. When we pulled up to her home after our trip, Jeff was waiting in the driveway for us. Before I could say anything, he gave Angie a big hug and told her how much he missed her, then said, "Okay, where's my present?" She pulled back, looked at him square in the face, and said, "Jeff, I'm your present! I came back!" He gave her another big hug and smile, and they walked into the house together.

Angie's favorite place to shop in Cooperstown is a little boutique owned by proprietors Wayne and L.J. They love seeing Angie, and we make it a point to go in and say hello whether we are shopping or just visiting. It's mostly a clothing, shoe, and accessory store, but occasionally they have a few pieces of vintage dishware or glassware for sale. One Saturday during a visit, the store was pretty busy. As we made our way around the store reviewing all the lovely clothing items and accessories, Angie found a sectioned porcelain hors d'oeuvres plate in a silver carrier. She took one look at it and said, "I want that!" I said, "Angie, honey, that seems like a lot of money (thirty-six dollars), and you really don't use anything like that at home." She was not deterred. She said again that she wanted it. As I started to say something else, she picked it up and marched to the counter and set it down in front of Wayne. "I want this," she told him. I walked up right behind her, but there were already five people lined up behind her waiting to check out. Wayne looked at me as she started fumbling in her purse for her money. She laid a couple of twenty-dollar bills on the counter, then started explaining to everyone around her, "This be-you-ti-ful dish, it's good for parties, it's good for snacks; you can put your peanuts in there and your olives in there! And it's so good for entertaining!" Then she wheeled around to the five people fidgeting in line behind her and said, "And—I'm very entertaining!" Everyone chuckled. Wayne looked at her with a big smile. "Angie," he said, "today this dish is on special, just for you! Twenty dollars!" There were lots of smiles in the crowded store as we left, Angie with her entertaining dish wrapped and ready to take home.

Bob and I loved it in Cooperstown and usually traveled there three times a year. In the late spring by ourselves, in August with my dad, Angie, and occasionally Joe, and in the fall again by ourselves. We would spend about three weeks there in the fall and the spring. In the spring of 2017, while enjoying our last few days before heading home, we got a call on a Thursday night from Angie. "You need to be home on Saturday by six o'clock!" she blurted immediately after we said hello. "Honey," I reminded her, "we're in New York." "I know," she said, "but it's for my recital!" "Recital? What recital?" we asked. "It's a surprise," she said. "I'm taking ballet, and I have a recital on Saturday night! You have to come!" It indeed was a surprise, the first we had heard of it.

We decided we had better get in gear and make a flying trip. We closed the house, packed quickly, and left early the next morning. We had become accustomed to spending two nights on the road when making the trip, but not this time! We arrived at our house at 4 p.m. Saturday, threw our luggage in the house, grabbed a bite to eat, stopped and got a bouquet of flowers, and arrived at the theater by 5:30 p.m. After buying tickets and settling in our seats, I decided to get up and get closer to the stage to see if I could get a picture when Angie came out. We could see from the program that there were four groups ranging in age from toddlers to adults performing ahead of her. The adult dancers were last on the program. When her group came out, it took my breath away. The costumes were exquisite! She looked like a princess. As Angie reached her mark, I saw her bend from the waist with her hands over her eyes, looking around the theater. Through the glare of the stage lights, she was searching for us. I was so glad that we had made it! The picture I took of her in that searching pose has remained one of our favorites. We thought the performance was beautiful, but more importantly, it was something she chose to do for herself. She decided to dance.

The organization that arranged the recital, DanceAbility, was started by a physical therapist named Jennifer several years ago in conjunction with the Missouri Contemporary Ballet (now Mareck Center for Dance) in Columbia, Missouri. Jennifer had taken a ballet class and happened to find out that a young friend of hers named Olive who had Down syndrome was also taking a class there. The wheels started turning when the instructor asked Jennifer if she had any advice for her about how to adapt some of her instruction and some of the moves for this student. The idea of an adaptive ballet class was born, and different age groups were added to the classes as time went on. The adult class was added a year or two before Angie joined. DanceAbility now consists of five or six different age groups. A group of physical therapists and others volunteer, along with the ballet artists from the company who serve as choreographers and instructors. After each twelve-week course, a recital is held for families and friends to see their loved ones perform. These festive recitals are usually packed, and flowers are handed out to each dancer after the recital. The cheers and bravos after each performance could equal those at the Metropolitan Ballet. Everyone, regardless of ability, deserves the opportunity to keep dancing in life and wear beautiful costumes. When I think of what it has given Angie, it makes my heart smile. It has added another layer of grace and accomplishment to her life. You can see it in her movements and in her face.

Angie and Jeff's love and friendship lasted for several years. Jeff was a few years older than Angie. When he began having health problems and moved to another more accommodating home in the Woodhaven system, you could tell that Angie was concerned about his health and the change she saw in him. Still, Woodhaven enabled them to be together, visiting back and forth and seeing each other at group events. She talked to us about him whenever she was home with us. We could hear the concern in her voice. Jeff's health took a gradual downturn, and he passed away when we were in New York during the fall. There was no way that we could make it back in time to be with her at the memorial service. Joe came over from St. Louis to be with her and lend his support and comfort. All Woodhaven was at the service for this sweet gentleman, along with family, community friends, and some local TV celebrities whom Jeff had befriended through the years. Many got up and spoke about their friendships with Jeff, telling humorous stories about their time with him. Angie decided that she wanted to say something. She was escorted up to the podium, and her spoken words were short but memorable. "Jeff was my man. He was a hot mess, and now he's gone. I will miss him." She mourned Jeff, but in her usual way, she walked back into her life routine, remembering Jeff with a star in the night sky a few weeks later.

My dad, Angie's Jiddo, died in 2018. She had seen him almost every day since 2009, when she started work at Tiger Place. He had been diagnosed with rapidly progressing Alzheimer's. It was a difficult end to the messy trajectory of his last few years. His wonderful physician, Dr. Paul, helped make his transition to hospice and his transition to his life's end as seamless as possible.

I worried during that time what would happen if Dad died at Tiger Place. Would Angie's grief affect her ability to continue her work there? She loved her job and felt so connected to all of the staff and residents. Because of his escalating care and safety needs, Dad ultimately had to leave Tiger Place and go to an Alzheimer's assisted living facility where he lived the last six months of his life. We were saddened but thankful at the same time.

We started noticing that Angie had developed a slight limp. She was taken to a well-respected orthopedic physician who X-rayed her knee and prescribed an elastic knee brace. I asked the doctor about physical therapy (PT). He laughed and said no, it wouldn't do any good. The fact that he laughed and appeared to patronize her irritated me to no end. She wore the brace, but it didn't seem to do anything to help her. We noticed her knee turning in more and more over the next few months. I was talking with another nurse one day, and she suggested we get an X-ray of Angie's hip. I asked her primary care doctor to order the X-ray. It turned out that Angie had a necrotic hip joint.

Bob and I took her for an evaluation to the Rehab Institute of Chicago (recently renamed the Shirley Ryan AbilityLab). This is where my brother Mike had practiced before he passed away, and some of his friends still worked there. Her evaluation showed that a lot of her limp was caused by muscle weakness in the hip. They prescribed a specific course of PT and exercises to strengthen her hip muscles so that she could avoid surgery for a while. We made her exercises a priority whenever we were together. Tiger Place had long hallways arranged in a big square. Before work a couple of times a week, Angie would walk sideways, left hip leading and then right hip leading, all around the square. We would take her over on Sundays to do the same. It worked for several years until her mobility and pain level started to affect her ability to work.

When it was apparent that we could not put the surgery off any longer, we had to figure out who to take her to. Someone who would do the best job for her. We knew that her mobility would greatly affect her quality of life. Angie was someone who loved her life of social activities, dancing, friends, work, and volunteering. We didn't want any of that to change. I decided to ask some physical therapists and home health nurses that I knew the following questions: Who was the hip surgeon with the best outcomes? Who had the best overall plan of care? And who was the easiest to get in contact with when needed? Everyone I asked told me it was Dr. Alan. It was a six-month wait until Angie could get an appointment. Since he was at a different hospital than her primary physician, Dr. Alex, I picked up her records and hand-carried them over to his office with our handwritten letter of explanation and request for his services. A week later I got a call saying he would be happy to take her case. We made the appointment and waited, praying that nothing would go wrong in the meantime. Her choice was to continue to work. We didn't push the issue because she had a housekeeping cart that she leaned on to wheel around. We did not want her to become deconditioned from lack of activity. Her surgery was set for March 6, 2020.

We again did our best to prepare Angie both mentally and physically for the surgery. We rejoiced with her every chance we got, telling her that she was getting a "brand spanking new hip!" This new hip would help her walk and dance and feel a lot better. We prepared her to be excited instead of afraid. We knew fretting in front of her would serve no positive purpose. We worried quietly about her heart and her cognition, which might be affected by a general anesthetic. Angie was forty-six when she had the surgery. Past the age of forty is a time when there can be concerns about the chromosomal link between Down syndrome and Alzheimer's disease.

In January of 2020, we started hearing more about something called Covid-19, a virus that had descended on the United States. The news just kept getting worse and worse. I think we all expected it to dissipate in a month or two, but it didn't. We watched, very concerned about Angie's surgery date. The thought of her in the hospital for any length of time was concerning. Still, we went ahead with the surgery, thinking that she would be there three days or so. Dr. Alan was aware of her heart conditions, and her cardiologists were informed and on call for the surgery. It went better than we could ever have hoped. Her heart was never an issue, and she walked three hundred feet on her "brand spanking new hip" the day of surgery! She came home the next day with a big smile on her face. The day of her homecoming, all elective surgeries at that hospital were shut down because of Covid. We had just made the cutoff.

Pain expression is something that I feel I need to touch on here. We had great difficulty figuring out if she was hurting and how much. She did not respond to the word "pain." When asked if she was in pain, it was as if she was afraid to admit it. We finally got results when we started being more specific and using other words that were not so threatening. "Is your knee wonky today?" always yielded better results than "Are you in pain?" for more generalized pain. I got results with an adapted pain scale that looked like a thermometer. We substituted Angie-adapted words for the numbers. She has never responded to the word pain so we used words along the scale like "no hurt," "a little hurt," and "a whole lot of hurt!" I know it will be different for everyone, but it has improved communication between Angie, her healthcare workers and us. I also had success after her hip replacement by asking her periodically if she wanted a pill to make her hip feel better. Asking if her hip was painful didn't quite get the job done with her.

Since she had just had the surgery and Covid was in full swing, she came to stay with Bob and me while she recuperated. PT came to the house, and Angie was to get out of her chair and walk around our house every hour. She was able to continue her ballet lessons with DanceAbility on Zoom. She looked forward to her 5:30 p.m. lesson every Thursday. She would stand with her walker watching the instruction on my tablet and follow along with her exercises.

We figured Angie would be with us maybe three weeks at the most. Because of Covid and the fact that she was having her bathroom remodeled, it was over two months before Angie went home. I wondered how hard it would be on her to disrupt her routine by keeping her for that period of time, but she endured it with grace and love. We did what we could to have fun. We took rides in the country, put puzzles together, watched movies, FaceTimed with her roommates and some of her cousins, painted pictures, cooked together, and did exercises. Before we let her go back, we checked into policies dealing with Covid in the Woodhaven homes. Support staff were to wear a mask at all times. Clients wore masks while in common areas but could remove them when alone in their own rooms. These policies proved effective. While these policies could only be enforced during working hours, we feel it definitely saved Angie from getting Covid, even with a few exposures from mask-wearing staff. We allowed Angie to return home three weeks after she was able to get her second Covid vaccine.

Again, we thought Covid would slow down in the coming months, but it did not. During October, I started to wonder what it might be like if Angie got it and could not come home over the holidays. Bob and I talked long about it and made the decision in October to pull her out of Woodhaven for a while. They were doing nothing wrong, but we did not want to take a chance. Bob's younger brother Jim had just died of Covid, and with Angie's heart problems, it was clear to us that she was at great risk for serious complications or worse. The day she was to come home, we found out another staff member had Covid and Angie had again been exposed. We were delayed by several days but with great relief brought her home at the beginning of November. Having her home for holiday preparation was a joy. We explained why she had to come home, and she patiently accepted the change, knowing that at some point she would go back to her former life and activities. We knew how much she understood when one day we were out for a ride. We drove by the normally packed but now totally empty parking lot of a local store. Bob remarked, "Look at that!" Angie answered, "Yah, it's because of Covid!"

While Angie was staying with us during the onset of Covid, I received a call from a young journalism school student reporter from our local NBC affiliate. Matt, we found out, had a twin brother who had Down syndrome. He had seen a post I had made on Facebook about our concerns for Angie after her hip replacement. He wanted to interview our family about how Covid had impacted our lives, especially Angie's. After Matt offered assurances that he would double-mask, we agreed to let him come. He brought his TV camera and spent about four hours with us that day talking to Angie, Bob, and me. He filmed us talking, Angie dancing (after her hip replacement), and Angie working on her puzzles that Joe had given her for Christmas.

When we saw the piece on the news, we were amazed at how well it captured both our hope and our concern for her future. We immediately started hearing from family and friends in town who had seen and loved the broadcast piece. Matt sent us the link, and we sent it on to family and friends. An affiliate from Springfield picked up the piece, and it aired in the southern part of the state as well. Our biggest surprise was that a friend who had moved to the Netherlands contacted me shortly after—they followed the news from Columbia and had seen the piece on the internet.

We have a dear friend, Jenny, who is an accomplished and talented artist. She is a young woman but went through breast cancer a couple of years before I did. This fact and the fact that we truly enjoyed each other's company cemented our friendship. I had a few of her smaller pieces but always wanted something bigger, commissioned just for our family. While Angie was with us recuperating from her hip replacement, we would make her get up and walk around the house every hour or so. When she did, she had a routine that she would follow. She would stop at each painting or print on the wall and study it. We would hear her mumble things like "Wow!" or "I like that!" I bought her some paints, colored pencils, and some pads. She loved drawing and coloring. One day I complimented her on what she was working on. "Angie, you are an artist!" Her reply, "I know a real artist! Her name is Jenny!" made me think. Wouldn't it be fun to have them collaborate on something? Maybe the whole family could!

We pitched the idea to Jenny. The process would be that Bob and Joe would come up with words to describe our family, and Angie would help Jenny lay on the foundation and choose and apply some of the base colors. She could also write anything into the base that she chose. On the appointed day, we went to Jenny's house. It was a beautiful day, and Jenny had everything ready for us on her covered back porch. Angie was in awe as Jenny explained the process to her and what her part would be. And it began. Jenny mixed the colorless base material and had Angie spread it on the board from corner to corner (I got to help with this part!).

Angie took her time, using her hands in a rhythmic motion, back and forth, spreading it in small curving waves. When it was satisfactory to her, she used her finger to slowly write our names—Bob, De, Angie, Joe. She then glossed over the names with more subtle curves and told Jenny it was time to add the color. The look on her face was a priceless mixture of joy and confidence in her role. Jenny told her to pick up any color she wanted for the base coat of paint. She used several and worked the paint in with a brush, again in waves across the board. David, Jenny's husband, filmed the event, and Bob and I took pictures.

When we reached the point where Jenny would take over and finish the painting, David suggested we all go for a boat ride on the lake their property adjoins. A perfect ending to the day. Jenny would finish the painting from that point and contact us in about three weeks. The descriptive words from Bob and Joe would be woven into the painting, along with sea glass we had gathered from Curaçao on a trip to see our cousins who live on that beautiful island, and crushed pearls from Jenny.

The finished product was so beautiful! It captured the love our family has for one another. Jenny, also knowing my love of trees, wove the words "loving," "loyal," "caring," "supporting," and "helping" into the branches of the large main subject of the painting. For Christmas that year, we had Jenny make a print of the painting on metal for Angie so that she could have her own copy. Jenny included a beautiful personal note to her on the back. Jenny told us she loved working with Angie!

We at one time thought about filing for guardianship of Angie. We talked with her doctor and again talked with an attorney about what this would look like. In the end, we decided not to do it but just to continue as her durable power of attorney. Since she was capable of doing so, we wanted her to be able to vote and participate in her own decision making as fully as possible. In Angie's case, guardianship would interfere with her ability to do this. It has worked well for all of us.

We received a call from a former Woodhaven employee several weeks before some recent state elections. Leigh Ann works for a state advocacy group for people who are differently abled. They were making an instructional video that would be sent to all voting places statewide and would be used to help voters with special physical or cognitive needs use the voting machines. She asked us if we would mind if Angie acted in the video. We said if Angie wanted to participate, it was fine with us. Angie's roommate, Mendy, was also asked, and together they played the parts of the voter and the election worker. The video was great! We were amazed at how well they both acted and performed the specific voting tasks in the video. We are proud of the service the video continues to provide those who need extra instruction to vote in Missouri. The video is still available on YouTube.

CHAPTER 10
FOOD FOR THOUGHT

When both Angie and Joe were babies, I would set them in the kitchen in a baby rocker and talk to them while I cooked. I read recipes out loud to them and named ingredients and measurements as I added them to the pot or bowl. It always amazed me how much they paid attention. It was a cooking show with me dancing around the kitchen and a captive but happy audience. We recognized as they matured that Angie and Joe both loved to cook and help in the kitchen. As she got older, Angie would chop, stir, hold a mixer, and add premeasured ingredients with great flourish. These basic kitchen activities graduated as she grew to yield greater benefits than just help with preparation of food. Angie, who often had trouble with conversing and articulating events and feelings, talked and told me things as we cooked together. She talked about school, her friends, her school bus rides, and what she wanted to make for dinner tomorrow night. It was almost as if she needed to have a different part of her brain occupied in order to release the part that allowed her to articulate feelings and thoughts (taking walks with her also helps her open up). I really cherished these moments.

Angie's specialty became cutting up the fruit for our holiday fruit salad that Joe loved so much. Another specialty is the Chex Mix that she makes (her Taita's recipe) and gives out with the cookies we bake together every Christmas. A couple of years ago I also became involved with the organization Lasagna Love. Volunteer home chefs are matched with people who need a meal for any reason; they then deliver free, fresh, homemade lasagna. When visiting, Angie has been thrilled to help me chop the veggies for my homemade sauce. It continues to provide an opportunity for us to talk about what is going on in her life.

As an adult in supported living, she loves to cook! Since Angie loves to eat, good nutrition and food intake has been a constant concern. We have struggled trying to find a way to help her know what good nutrition is. We settled on a very simple formula that had been the basis for a book that I read years ago. Five vegetables and fruits every day, a little bit of meat/protein, whole grains, and not too much sugar. I've tried to help her minimize processed foods but still struggle with how to define them for her. The five fruits and vegetables concept has become another lifelong mantra. Over the years, she has asked teachers, friends, relatives, Woodhaven executives, local TV personalities, doctors, etc. if they eat their five fruits and vegetables every day. Does she always follow this guideline consistently? Of course not, but the knowledge of what she should do is ingrained.

One memorable encounter that shows how little control we as parents have over our kids occurred after Angie had moved out and was in supported living. She was telling me about a trip out to eat to a local chain restaurant with her staff and friends. I asked what she had ordered to eat. "The Trio," she effused (a feast that consists of a platter of ribs, chicken, and shrimp). Suddenly all the healthy food-related teaching I had tried to do with her came flooding back into my head and smacked the mom lecture button! I launched into a diatribe about food choices and health, portion size, overeating, etc., etc. I did this with an open right palm, slapping it with the side of my left hand. I went on until the thoughts in my head had emptied and I took a breath. Angie had not taken her eyes off me. "Now do you understand what I am telling you about your food choices next time?" I asked. She hesitated, looked at me, and said, "Uhhhh, just get the ribs?"

Food is a cultural phenomenon that is different for each person and family. I grew up without fried foods or many processed foods (except for white rice!). My family is both Lebanese and Palestinian, and we integrated many ethnic recipes into our diet growing up. Bob, who grew up in south Missouri, was raised on biscuits and gravy and two or more starches at every meal. While he loves Middle Eastern food and the less starchy meals we eat now, the craving for fried fish will never leave him (I love it too!). Thus is the rub with us and with every wonderful care partner who has ever come into Angie's life. We all have different ideas of what good, healthy food means.

So how do we solve this? We don't, but we do keep trying to educate and provide opportunities to improve the balance of foods that Angie consumes. There are healthy recipes from home that Angie loved growing up. I have provided staff a few recipes, some ethnic, that are simple enough that they can cook together. I'll never forget the first time one of the staff decided to give one of the dishes a try. It was a dish called lubiyeh, a Lebanese recipe consisting of lean ground beef or lamb and green beans (I also add sliced fresh mushrooms) in a savory tomato sauce seasoned with garlic, cinnamon, salt, and pepper and served over brown rice. When I sent this recipe, I knew it was something they were not familiar with and wondered if they would give it a try. It was simple to make, but the seasoning combination would be odd to someone not used to it. One afternoon several months after I sent it, I got a text from one of Angie's staff members saying, "I had to step away from taste-testing this since there needed to be enough for dinner tonight! I am just amazed at the flavor combination!" Included was a cute picture of a very proud Angie holding the pot of lubiyeh up for the camera.

The following is a recipe for our family's version of lubiyeh:

Lubiyeh Ingredients:
    1 to 1 1/2 lbs of 90% lean ground sirloin
    1 15-oz can of Hunt's no salt added diced tomatoes (any canned diced tomatoes will work)
    1 28-oz can of Dei Fratelli no salt added crushed tomatoes (any canned crushed tomatoes will work)
    1 16-oz package of frozen green beans
    8 oz of fresh baby belle mushrooms, sloshed around in several changes of water to clean, then air dried and sliced
    1 1/2 tsp of salt
    1 1/2 tsp of garlic powder
    1/3 tsp of cinnamon
    pepper to taste
    parmesan cheese to taste (optional)
    whole grain rice (suggested recipe below)

Directions:
    In a 6-quart saucepan, add ground sirloin and season with pepper, garlic, cinnamon, and 1 tsp salt. Sauté over medium heat until meat is done. Add green beans, season with rest of salt and a little pepper, and cook with meat for a few minutes. Add diced tomatoes and crushed tomatoes. Fill the large can halfway with water. Pour back and forth in the tomato cans to rinse, then add to the pot. Stir well to mix. Bring to a boil over medium heat. When it starts boiling, add the raw sliced mushrooms and stir. Turn down, partially cover, and simmer for 45 minutes to an hour, stirring occasionally. Adjust seasoning to

taste. Serve over whole grain rice. We also like a sprinkle of parmesan cheese over the top when it is plated. This is actually better the next day.

Rice Ingredients:
1 1/2 cups of Uncle Ben's whole grain brown rice (or your favorite brand)
1/4 cup of orzo or thin spaghetti broken in approximately 1 1/2-inch lengths
2 tsp of olive oil
2 1/2 cups of water
salt & pepper to taste

Directions:
Put oil in saucepan and heat on low. Add orzo or spaghetti pieces and sauté until slightly brown. Add rice and sauté, stirring until the rice starts browning and has a nutty smell. This should take just a few minutes. Add water and salt, then stir. Turn up heat to medium. When it starts to boil, reduce heat to low and keep covered. Check after about 25 minutes by tipping the pan to see if there is water in the bottom. If it looks dry, add a couple of tablespoons of water and cover. You can taste a couple of kernels of rice to see if it's done. Put the lid back on and let set a couple of minutes. Stir up and serve with the sauce.

Both of our children were very close to both sets of their grandparents. My parents happened to live in the same neighborhood we did, while

Bob's parents moved to south Missouri when Angie was about ten and Joe eight. Self-talk is a common phenomenon in the world of people with Down syndrome. Self-talk has been shown to be a normal and useful adaptation of thought processes that helps them understand and weigh decisions, complete thoughts, commit things to memory, work through dilemmas, and give themselves encouragement.

As an example, when my mother was about to turn sixty, we decided to have a surprise party for her. We told Angie about it and impressed upon her that it was a surprise and not to say a word. We knew we were in trouble when Angie started walking around the house wide-eyed, repeating, "Don't tell Taita about her birthday party, don't tell Taita about her birthday party, don't—!" We tried putting our finger up to our lips and saying, "Shush!" when we heard her say this, but that just got added to her self-talk. So then it was, "Angie, shush! Don't tell Taita about her birthday party—!" We finally just gave up, knowing it was a matter of time until Taita found out. The next time we were at Mom and Dad's house, Angie saw my mom when we walked in the front door. She looked straight at her Taita and repeated, "Don't tell Taita about her birthday party—Oh shoot, ANGIE! You're not supposed to say that!" All we could do was laugh and then ask my mother what kind of cake she wanted.

CHAPTER 11
A FULL LIFE

There were times when both Bob and I mourned having a child with a genetic anomaly that would make her different from most other children and adults. We were never at our low points at the same time. We realize that parents can mourn any number of things about their children. We all have expectations, however realistic or unrealistic. We love them for who they are and for all the joys, heavy and light moments, enigmas and wonders, perplexities and confounding complexities, and surprises that they bring us. Angie is really no different than any other child on the spectrum of life and living. We would not trade either of our children for anything more or different.

You might be curious what Angie's life looks like today. We can honestly say that Woodhaven has partnered with Angie to enable her to have a wonderful life. Angie and her roommate, Mendy, continue to share a duplex with two other Woodhaven housemates next door in the Columbia, Missouri, community. Angie and Mendy have been together since 1997. Her friends Lucy and Sarah have been next door for several years. Angie works in housekeeping at the same job she has had since 2009. Because she might be at risk of losing her Medicaid/Medicare insurance along with her disability SSI, she can only work from 9 a.m. to 12 p.m. four days a week. With her medical history, her insurance and SSI serve as a lifeline that she cannot afford to lose. Angie and her roommates volunteer for Meals-on-Wheels on Fridays.

For many years, Angie has loved participating in three six-week sessions yearly of therapeutic horseback riding at Cedar Creek Riding Center. She wouldn't miss her three times yearly, twelve-week sessions of DanceAbility ballet. We hope she never stops dancing. Thanks to her friend Reverend Sally, Angie for many years has been very involved in Aktion Club, an extension of Kiwanis Club for people with special needs. She has been an Aktion Club member, board member, vice president, and president (she loves the titles!). Aktion Club members vote on and carry out yearly community projects such as food drives and other fund raisers that help sustain the community at large.

She participates in Clean-Up-Columbia. She can also be found each March working at the Kiwanis Pancake Breakfast. She does find time to spend most Sundays and holidays with us and remains very close to her brother, Joe, and his sweet dog, Lady. She talks with Joe every Sunday night. She loves our yearly trips to Cooperstown, New York, for our Hage Family Reunion on Otsego Lake.

We have reached a period in Angie's life where we need to start thinking about what the future will hold for her as she ages. It's not uncommon now with our medical advancements for people with Down syndrome to live well into their 60s and 70s. We are navigating the end of her 40s as I write this. A big concern for us and others in the same boat is the link between Down syndrome and Alzheimer's disease. We have long subscribed to the theory that the only meaningful things we can really give our kids are love, guidance, opportunities, and experiences. In Angie's case, we try to continue presenting her with new experiences in the hopes that it will challenge her capacity to think and understand. As an example, this past Thanksgiving we took a family trip to Bentonville, Arkansas, to spend time at the Crystal Bridges Museum. We visited other museums in town, walked the long trails, and enjoyed a nighttime outdoor interactive exhibit. She loved it all. The St. Louis Zoo is a favorite, and she has enjoyed trips to the Butterfly House in St. Louis and the Nelson-Atkins Museum of Art in Kansas City. She loves going to movies and concerts of all kinds, and free music venues around Columbia. A trip to the Arab American Museum in Dearborn, Michigan, surprised all of us. She looked with awe at every single exhibit. A couple of years ago we took a trip to Yellowstone and the Grand Tetons with her. She told me later that sometimes the clouds in the sky look like geysers.

The question that follows is, what comes next after years of successfully being in supported living, if and when Angie can no longer be cared for in her current environment. Woodhaven has a few designated homes for their medically fragile clients and has wisely partnered with hospice for some of their clients at the end of their lives. This extends the ability of their clients to stay in a comfortable, familiar system that understands the care needs, wishes, and habits of the individuals who are served. Of course, there are still things that need to be adapted or worked out to improve end-of-life care in this setting. There are no perfect places, but Woodhaven has done a great job so far of enabling the lives of people with special needs at all levels of life.

We are making big plans for Angie's fiftieth birthday as I finish writing her story. It'll be another big bash with music, fun, and food. Thinking about this, I cannot help but ponder two different quotes that Bob rendered after we had looked back on two different and difficult times of our lives. They signify our maturation and growth occurring through the process of raising our family:

"Before she was born, I prayed for a perfect child. It took me a while to realize we got exactly what I asked for."

"Sometimes the worst day of your life can make the best days of the rest of your life."

The above quotes really apply to all our children at one time or another. Both of our kids are busy adults. Angie still only has time to love us on Sunday.

Angie's match at International Special Olympics, 1995

Angie with her flowers after her first recital

Helping me make my home-made lasagna sauce for Lasagna Love deliveries

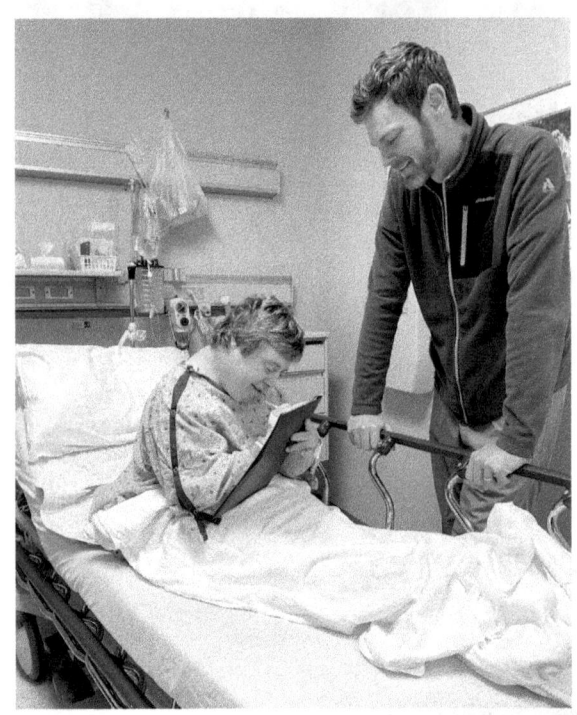

Surgeon Dr. "Alan" watching while Angie signs her permission slip for her hip replacement

Angie after a hard day at Yellowstone

Angie riding horseback at Cedar Creek Riding Stables

Angie and Joe with Joe's sweet new puppy Lady

Jenny and Angie on the day our family painting was started

Angie was so excited to work on this!

Angie and Jiddo playing checkers on the front porch of our house in Cooperstown, New York

Angie showing off a pot of lubiyeh

A recent DanceAbility picture of Angie and her roommate with PT Jennifer

Angie and two of her housmates in the van ready for adventure!

Angie wrote a book for her father for Father's Day.

ACKNOWLEDGMENTS

This book has been residing in my heart and my head for a very long time. The help and encouragement that I have received along the way will always be a part of me.

Thank you, Bob and Joe, for your insights, love, encouragement, and careful reading.

Thank you, Marie Hage Osborn, for reading my first paragraphs and urging me forward. And my sister-friend, Janis Tate, for reading my ending and understanding what I meant to convey. That was a light bulb moment for me.

Thank you Dr. Marilyn Rantz RN, PhD, FAAN, for giving me the opportunity to learn to tell a story when you hired me so many years ago. Some of those thousands of pages of fieldnotes are still etched in my mind.

Thank you to my St. George Ladies Book Club. Your love and support have been a blessing.

I cannot tell you how humbled I was when the much-lauded Steve Weinberg generously offered to read the manuscript that he had encouraged me to write a few years ago. Your advice was invaluable and so much appreciated. Thank you again, Steve!

Last, but certainly not least, Thank you Yolanda Ciolli from Compass Flower Press. I could not have done this without your encouragement, advice, patience, and help!

This book was written at the Daniel Boone Public Library, and The Grind coffee house on John Garry Drive, both in Columbia, Missouri.

WOODHAVEN GALA SPEECH 2011

A PARENT'S PERSPECTIVE ON WOODHAVEN,
DELIVERED BY DE MINNER

Good Evening! It's wonderful to see everyone. We are blessed to have the children that we have, and tonight we celebrate the successful lives of all who are served by Woodhaven.

When I was asked to talk this evening about a parent's perspective on Woodhaven, I had to go back and think a little about the role of a parent. I believe our role as a parent is to love, nurture, protect, and to encourage independence. These are all pretty tough things at times, but that last one, encouraging independence—it can be a killer when you have a child with challenges and your first inclination is to protect.

Over the last several years, I have had the opportunity to meet and share stories with mothers and female relatives of individuals served by Woodhaven at a yearly Mother's Day luncheon. What seems to be a continuing theme in these stories is the realization that, as parents, we are often so busy loving and caring for our children that we don't see what is possible for them until someone else shows us. And, no matter how wonderful we are as parents, we can't provide that needed level of independence by ourselves, because to us, they will always be our children.

So, we need another pair of eyes to help us see our children, as adults, in light of their potential. And we need a trustworthy partnership to enable our adult children to be the best that they can be, to live the best and happiest lives that they can live—as adults!

I know that for many of us, Woodhaven has lovingly provided that partnership, shown us the possible, and helped our loved ones achieve the goals of a happy life. Isn't that what success is all about, being happy? For Angie, those goals include her living independently with a job that she loves, and spending time with the activities that satisfy and stimulate her interests.

Is it a perfect partnership? No, there is no such thing. But—for Bob, me, and Joe, it is a wonderful dynamic partnership that includes all of us, with Angie right smack in the middle. She *IS* living a very happy life. Thank you!

WHAT IS DOWN SYNDROME?

Approximately six thousand babies are born with Down syndrome (DS) every year in the United States, and one hundred thousand worldwide. Occurring at a rate of about one in seven hundred live births, it is considered one of the most common congenital anomalies. Although most mothers of babies born with DS are of normal childbearing age, the incidence of DS births goes up with the age of the mother at birth.

Most of us are born with 23 pairs of chromosomes on which our genetic makeup (our genes) is loaded. These 46 chromosomes occur in each cell in our body. These genes are the reason we are each an individual with unique characteristics.

Down syndrome is caused by one of three different changes in chromosomal structure that start at conception when the first human cells divide and continue through the growth of all cells before birth. These changes are referred to as trisomy 21, translocation, or mosaicism.

Trisomy 21, accounting for 95 percent of births with Down syndrome, occurs when an extra 21st chromosome appears in each cell. The two other types of chromosomal changes account for a very small percentage of DS. Translocation occurs when a piece of chromosome 21 breaks off and attaches to another chromosome. This mixture then replicates itself in every cell. Mosaicism occurs when only some of the cells have an extra copy of the 21st chromosome and many normal cells replicate alongside the affected cells. Although very rare, a small percentage of parents of children with translocation Down syndrome can be considered genetic carriers. There is no evidence of this with either trisomy 21 or mosaic Down syndrome.

Several related health problems can occur along with Down syndrome. The following are some of the major ones, although it's good to keep in mind that these do not occur with every DS birth: heart defects, lax joints, decreased muscle tone, ear infections, slow cognitive development, and atlantoaxial instability.

It's also important to keep in mind that medical care for people with Down syndrome has greatly improved during the last several years. The Global Down Syndrome Foundation offers global medical care guidelines for people with Down syndrome from infancy through adulthood. They are available in formats for both healthcare providers and laypeople. These guidelines are free and can be accessed at the web address below.

https://www.globaldownsyndrome.org

With good medical care, most people with Down syndrome can live a long, active, and happy life.

www.ingramcontent.com/pod-product-compliance
Lightning Source LLC
Chambersburg PA
CBHW070159100426
42743CB00013B/2979